The Tru

TULUM

Including:
The Bizarre Events,
Weird Connections,
Wacky Theories, &
Offbeat Characters
of Tulum

....

Everything you need to know
before you go to the ruins,
- or -
What you wish you read
before you went!

In 1985, during a project carried out by the *Instituto Nacional de Antropología e Historia (INAH)* and funded by a grant from the National Geographic Society, Ric Hajovsky paddled a dugout canoe over the reef to land on the beach at Tulum, in an effort to test the theory that El Castillo was a Maya lighthouse. Later, he traveled the coast of Panama all the way from the border of Costa Rica south to Colombia in *Don Tiki*, his 45-foot-long, ocean-going dugout which was similar to the type the Maya used to carry trade-goods from as far north as Tabasco to as far south as Honduras. Read more about Ric and his archaeological and ethnographical adventures in Mexico, Panama, Suriname, Amazonian Peru, and Spain, by visiting his web site: **www.EverythingCozumel.com**

Other books written by Ric are:

- *The True History of Cozumel*

- *Historia Verdadera de Cozumel (en español)*

- *The Yellow Guide to the Mayan Ruins of San Gervasio, Cozumel*

- *Cozumel Survival Manual*

- *Mexico Survival Manual*

- *December 21, 2012: Everything you need to know to understand what all the fuss is about*

- *The Lost Kivas of San Lazaro*

- *The True and Faithful Account of the Adventures of Trader Ric in Kuna Yala*
- *The True and Faithful Account of the Adventures of Trader Ric on the Trail of Cristóbal Colon*
- *The True and Faithful Account of the Adventures of Trader Ric at the Headwaters of the Tapanahonie*
- *The True and Faithful Account of the Adventures of Trader Ric in the Darien Gap*
- *Spain: Hidden Secrets and Dirty Tricks; how to travel in Spain in high style, but at a budget price*
- *You Can't Get There From Here!*

Above: Sylvanus Griswold Morley, the US spy/archaeologist who worked in Tulum and was the man on whom the film character of Indiana Jones was based.

Contents

Above: Google Earth© image of the archaeological zone of Tulum.

Introduction

If you are reading this book, you are probably either planning on visiting Tulum, or just got back from a tour of the site. Either way, what you will read next is an account of the history of the walled city that is <u>not</u> covered by the tour guides. This is the <u>true</u> history of Tulum, without all the fables, hyperbole, garbled stories, and fairy-tales that so often find their way into the tour-guides' lectures. The book is designed to give you a thorough understanding of Tulum's past and armed with this knowledge, you will enjoy your tour that much more.

Today, Tulum is the second most visited archaeological site on the Yucatán Peninsula, following close behind Chichen Itzá. This, however, is a fairly recent turn of events. It was not all that long ago that Tulum was still a difficult place to travel to without a bush-plane, or a friend with a fishing boat!

Many years ago, I bought a small paper-back guide to Tulum. The foreword that appeared in that booklet, printed in 1968, can give you an idea of how much this coast has grown since then. The foreword read:

"At present one can reach Tulum directly from Merida by special plane or by a fishing boat from Cozumel. A new road is being planned which will connect Tulum with the Merida-Puerto Juarez highway [remember, this was before Cancun was built]. *Whether the journey is undertaken by air or by sea, it is possible to visit Tulum and return to Merida or to Cozumel the same day, but the visitor should take with him his food and beverages. However, those wishing to remain longer at Tulum can spend the night at the neighboring coconut ranch of Tancah."*

The man who wrote that booklet was Alberto Ruz Lhuillier, a Mexican government archaeologist. The text was a dry description of the structures on the site and a rendition of the theories of the day, but it didn't really delve into the real history of Tulum.

Above: Alberto Ruz Lhuillier, the author of the first guide I read on Tulum and INAH's Southern Director of Pre-Hispanic Monuments at the time.

By 1972, when the Merida-Puerto Juarez road (now highway) was first paved, the town of Tulum Pueblo had grown to an astounding 265 souls. Once the highway was open the age of "multi-national archaeo-tourism" began in earnest. However, the Maya living in the area did not want to have anything to do with these new visitors. They felt the tourists were a bad influence on their children and they kept their distance. When the Mexican government told them that they would train them to make handicrafts to sell to the tourists and that they build a new artisan market for them to sell the items, the Maya politely refused. They were more interested in continuing their old way of life, farming their *milpas* and gathering chicle. Consequently, the government transplanted people from the states of Guerrero and Yucatan to man the market and make souvenirs for the tourists. Years later, the Maya of Tulum Pueblo realized that they had lost a chance to make a better living, but it was too late.

Those days of camping out under the coconut palms are long gone, but Tulum is still a fascinating site. Today, millions of tourists arrive in Tulum aboard air-conditioned busses from Cancun and various points along the "Mayan Riviera." If you plan on being one of them, read up a little about the site before you go so you can get the most out of your trip.

Brief history of the Maya of the Yucatán peninsula

Small groups of the Paleo-Indians migrated south from the Bering Strait and established themselves temporarily in Yucatán as early as 14,000 years ago. Remains of these early New-World colonizers are just now beginning to turn up in the deep cenotes of Quintana Roo. The skeleton of the Paleo-Indian "Eve of Naharon" that was recently discovered in the Naranjal cave system near Tulum has been carbon-14 dated to 11,600 B.C., over 13,600 years ago. The 10,000-year-old remains of the Paleo-Indian "Mujer de La Palma" and the child "Joven de Chan Hol" that were just found near Tulum in Las Palmas cenote and Chan Hol cenote are just two of the other finds that have pushed back the timeline for the population of Quintana Roo.

These Paleo-Indians were only the forerunners of the human migration southward in the Americas. By 8,000 years ago, Archaic Period hunters and gatherers had populated Yucatán. Shortly thereafter, groups of these early settlers migrated out from northern Quintana Roo to settle the western portion of the Antilles and become the Casimiroid culture in Cuba, Puerto Rico, Hispaniola and other Antillean islands.

Around 4,500 years ago, during the Early Preclassic Period (also known as the Early Formative Period), the very beginnings of the Maya civilization began to coalesce and become what we now call the Proto-Maya. Within a few hundred years, these Proto-Maya begin to farm corn and their settlements become more permanent in nature.

By 2,300 years ago, the Late Preclassic (or Late Formative Period) began and more small settlements were established by a branch of the Maya we now call the Yucatec. These scattered settlements were supported mainly by hunting and small-plot agriculture, but writing, mathematics, and governmental systems began to be developed during this period. Over the next thousand years, their small villages grew into large cities and their system of government grew in complexity, as did their religion.

Another division of Maya, the Putún (sometimes called the Chontal-Putún) were living in Tabasco and southern Campeche at the time. These Putún Maya were accomplished seamen and had a well-established sea-trade route that ran all the way from the Gulf Coast of Mexico as far south as Honduras and as far east as the Antilles. These seafaring Maya were heavily influenced by their neighbors, the Toltecs and Mixtecs, both very warlike cultures.

Around 900 A. D., the Putún began to take over the territory of the Maya living in the Yucatán Peninsula, beginning with the island of Cozumel, where they had established trading posts earlier. Another faction of Putún entered from the west and Maya tradition asserts that group was led by a man-god whose name in nahuatl (the language of the Mixtec, Aztec, and Toltec) was Quetzalcoatl. The Maya called him Kukulcan and depicted him as a feathered serpent.

The Putún and their allies quickly subjected the Yucatec, and established themselves as the new ruling class of the peninsula, relegating the leaders of the Yucatec royal houses to positions subservient to Putún royal lineages. These newcomers became known in Yucatán as the Itzá. When they took over an older Yucatec city and rebuilt it in their own Toltec-influenced style, they renamed it Chichen Itzá and made it their capital. Along with new styles of architecture, the Itzá also introduced the bow and arrow and the Cult of Ixchel to the peninsula.

Possibly the first recorded mention of the Putún Maya trade routes was made by Fernando Colón, Cristóbal Colón's son, in which he recounted an event from his father's fourth and last voyage in his book, *Historie del S.D.Fernando Colombo; nelle quali s'ha particolare & vera relatione della vita & de'fatti dell'Almiraglio D. Christoforo Colombo suo padre*, which Fernando wrote between 1537 y 1539 before it was published in Venice in 1571. Fernando says that in Bonacca Cay in the Bay Islands of Honduras (called Guanaja by Colón), the Spaniards ran across a canoe full of the Indian traders bringing their wares to the inhabitants of the island. Fernando was also on that voyage, so what he wrote was an eyewitness account. An English translation of this account reads: *"Having come to the island of Guanaja, the Admiral sent ashore his brother Bartholomew, with two boats... by good fortune there arrived at that time a canoe, long as a galley and eight feet wide, made of a single tree trunk like the other Indian canoes; it was freighted with merchandise... amidships it had a palm-leaf awning like that on Venetian gondolas; this gave complete protection against the rain and waves. Underneath were women and children and all the baggage and merchandise. There were twenty-five paddlers aboard, but they offered no resistance when our boats drew up to them... He then ordered that there should be taken from the canoe whatever appeared to be most attractive and valuable, such as cloths and sleeveless shirts of cotton that had been worked and dyed in different colors and designs, also pantaloons of the same workmanship with which they cover their private parts, also cloth in which the Indian women of the canoe were dressed, such as the Moorish women of Granada are accustomed to wear. Also long swords of wood with a groove along each edge, wherein stone knives were set by means of fiber and pitch, cutting like steel when used on naked people; also hatchets to cut wood, like those of stone used by other Indians, save for the fact that these were of good copper, of which metal they also had bells and crucibles for smelting. For food they carried roots and grain such as they eat in Española and a certain wine made of maize, like the beer of England, and they had many of those kernels which serve as money in New Spain, which it appeared that they valued highly."* Most frequently this passage is quoted as proof that these were Maya whom Colón met in Bonacca, however, they could very well have been non-Maya Indians from that area (such as the Paya, Jicaque, or Mam) simply carrying on trade between the mainland of Honduras and the outer islands; there is no way to be sure.

Another account of the event was recorded by the early historian Peter Martyr d'Anghiera in his book *De orbe novo decades,* published in 1516. Martyr wrote that the canoe Colón saw was loaded with trade goods, like *"novaculae, cultelli, secures"* (large and small knives and cleavers) and ceramic cooking vessels.

Bartolomé de Las Casas also described Colón's encounter with the Indian traders in his book, *Historia de la Indias* written between 1527 and 1561. This is the English version of the account: *"...there came a canoe full of Indians, as long as a galley and eight feet in width; it came loaded with goods from the west and must certainly have been from the land of Yucatán, because it was close to there, a journey of 30 leagues or a little more; it was carrying in the middle of the canoe an awning of palm mats, which are called* petates *in New Spain, in and under which there came their women and children and property and goods, without the water from the sky nor the sea being able to wet the things. The goods and things that they were bringing were many cotton blankets, painted in many colors and designs, and sleeveless shirts, also painted and worked, and the* almaizares *which the men covered their private parts were also painted and worked... wood swords with grooved edges and certain flint blades attached with pitch and thread, copper hatchets for cutting wood and bells and some crucibles and patens for casting copper; many cacao* nuts, that they have for currency in New Spain and in Yucatán and elsewhere. *Their nourishment was corn bread and some edible roots that must have been those that we called* ajes *and* batatas *in Española and* camotes *in New Spain; their wine was also of corn, it looked like beer. There came in the canoe almost 25 men, and they did not venture to defend themselves nor did they flee the Christian ships...*" The fact that Las Casas added the line stating that he thought these Indian traders *"must certainly have been from the land of Yucatán"* simply because it was close by does not add any weight to that argument; it was only his personal opinion that he included in the description of the event, 25 years after it happened.

Bernal Díaz del Castillo described another group of the large Maya canoes that he saw while he was with Fernando de Córdoba on his 1517 voyage to Yucatán. In his book, *Historia Verdadera de la Conquista de la Nueva España*, Díaz says: *"On the morning of the fourth of March, five canoes came off to us. These vessels are like troughs, made of one entire tree and many of them capable of containing fifty men."*

Above: Engraving of a 54-man ocean-going canoe.

Hernán Cortés, in his 1526 "Fifth Letter" to the Spanish Crown, mentions how Spaniards in Tabasco and Xicalango were disrupting the flow of the traditional Maya sea trade routes: *"...there were certain Spaniards who did them much harm, for besides burning many villages and killing some of the inhabitants, as a result of which many of them abandoned those places and fled to the hills, they had most severely harmed the merchants and traders; for, because of them the trade which had once flourished along the coast had now ceased."*

Physical evidence of these trade routes is perhaps more reliable than these early texts. For example, a Taino Indian vomit spatula (used to induce vomiting during ritual cleansing ceremonies) was found in a Classic Period grave at Altun Ha, in Belize. Since the Taino occupied the Bahamas and the Greater and Lesser Antilles and were not known as traders, one would assume a Maya trader brought the ladle back with him to Belize from a sea voyage to one of those islands. On Antigua, a cache of Maya jadeite axes, or celts, was found in the 1990s. The origin of the jadeite from which these celts were crafted was the Motagua valley in Guatemala (1,800 miles away), as ascertained by mineralogist George Harlow, of the Museum of Antigua and Barbuda in St. John's, Antigua. Another group of Maya pottery shards and obsidian implements were found on the western tip of Cuba by Maurice Ries in the 1940s. In the 1980s, I personally found a Maya celt on a small islet off Highborn Cay, Bahamas, near an early Spanish shipwreck which I was excavating with the Institute of Nautical Archaeology. That celt also was made from jadeite that came from Guatemala.

Around 1000 A.D., the Itzá moved their capital to Mayapán and gathered the leaders of the other major Maya lordships in the Yucatán (the Tutul Xíu, Itzamal, and Cocom, as well as minor houses, like the Zamá ruling family, from Tulum) and kept them under their thumb as vassals in what we now call the League of Mayapán. The League lasted until the year 1194, when the Itzá were overthrown in a *coup-d'état*. The Cocom Maya took over the reins of power, but they were overthrown themselves by the Tutul Xíu Maya in 1411. From that point, until the arrival of the Spanish 100 years later, the *kuchkabals*, or independent Maya states of the peninsula, were constantly warring with first one neighbor and then another.

Pre-Conquest Tulum

Tulum was founded shortly after the fall of the Mayapán League; around the year 1200. It was because of the chaos and warfare between the *kuchkabals* that followed the demise of the League that the Maya of Tulum built a wall around their city. They were not the only Maya city to do so. Because the overland trade routes were severely disrupted by this warfare, the old sea-trade routes became even more important and the murals in Tulum showing ocean-going canoes arriving and departing attest to the fact that it became a prominent port city soon after its founding. Obsidian came to Tulum from Central Mexico, jade from Guatemala, copper from Honduras, and cacao beans from Tabasco; all to be trans-shipped in other canoes heading north and south. Business was good and for a while, Tulum thrived.

Each *kuchkabal* was ruled by a *halach uinik*, the hereditary chief of the major noble house. He laid down the policies regarding war, religion, and civil law. He was assisted by the *ah cuchcab*, a council made up of the *batabs* of the minor noble houses and the priests. The *bataboob* (Mayan plural of *batab*) were responsible for the enforcement of these policies within the communities that were presided over by their noble families. The *kuleloob* were the officials who ensured that the policies of the *halach uinik* were being enforced by the *bataboob*.

The *nacom* was the head of the army. During peacetime, he was subservient to the *halach uinik* of the leading noble house, but when the *halach uinik* declared war, he transferred his power to this expert. The *bataboob* of the minor houses also had *nacomoob*, as well as warriors who were loyal to them but who would all join together under an army led by the chief *nacom* if called upon.

The *tupiles* were the sheriffs. They kept an eye on the commoners. The *ah holpop* was the official in charge of the ceremonial dances and kept the villages musical instruments under his custody when not in use.

The priesthood was a hereditary position, called the *ah kin,* and passed from father to son. If no son was available to inherit, the title passed to the brother or nephew of the deceased priest. There were two kinds of priests: the *chilanoob*, or "speakers," who interpreted and passed on the gods' words and wishes, and the *nacom* (not to be confused with the war captain of the same name) who sliced open the sacrificial victim's chest and removed his beating heart.

Above: The *nacom* priest was the one in charge of the human sacrifices.

Maya religion

The Maya were polytheistic. Their lives were ruled by the will of the gods, as revealed to them through the priests. They believed in the immortality of the soul and in the concepts of heaven and hell. They believed that there were certain people who were guaranteed entrance to heaven: priests, women who died in childbirth, men who died in war, suicide victims, and people who were sacrificed to the gods. The Maya cosmological view was that the earth was a square plane, held up by the four *bacaboob*. Each *bacab* was associated with a cardinal point and a color: *Zac* was in the north and his color was white; *Kan* was in the south and his color was yellow; *Ek* was in the west and his color was black; *Chac* was in the east and his color was red. There were seven levels of heaven above the earth, each guarded by an *oxlahuntikú* and five regions of hell below, each guarded by a *bolontikú*. The lowest level of hell was *mitnal*, where Ah Puch, the god of death, ruled.

There were many other gods in their pantheon, such as Yumkaax, the corn god, and Kukulkán, the god of wind (also named Huracán, the root of our word hurricane). All these gods needed to be kept happy or the town would suffer. To insure the gods' happiness, the *chilanoob* would tell the people what the gods wanted. Sometimes it was abstinence, sometimes fasting, sometimes an offering, and sometimes a sacrifice.

Today, a few "new-age" believers carry flowers to some of the Maya temples, thinking that they are repeating a traditional act; making offerings to a god or goddess. It is difficult to imagine what the gods might make of this new kind of offering, but in times long past, flowers were not the gods' preferred gift. Diego de Landa mentions several kinds of animals sacrificed by the Maya, including dogs and deer. Furthermore, he describes human sacrifices which the pilgrims performed when they went to Cozumel: *"they have two unholy shrines of Chichen itzá and Cuzmil where they send an infinite number of unfortunates to be sacrificed or thrown from a height in one* [Chichen Itzá] *and the other* [Cozumel] *to have their hearts ripped out)."* Landa describes the human sacrifice thusly: *"The executioner priest arrived with a large stone knife and with practiced cruelty made a slash between the ribs, on the left side, under the nipple and then stuck his hand inside and tearing the heart out alive like a rabid tiger, and gave it to the priest on a plate, who then hurried and uncted the idols' faces with that fresh blood."* Landa continues, saying: *"...these sacrificial victims were commonly buried in the courtyard of the temple, or if they were not, they ate them, dividing them between the nobles and those who there was enough left over for."*

Guillermo de Anda, an archaeologist of the Autonomous University of Yucatán, performed an inventory of the bones of the victims of Maya sacrifices found submerged in the cenotes of Yucatán. He found that most of the skeletons were incomplete and disarticulated. He also stated that that most of those bones had butcher marks, pointing to the fact that the Maya ate the flesh of many of these victims. Some of these bones were also semi-carbonized, as if they had been roasted in a fire.

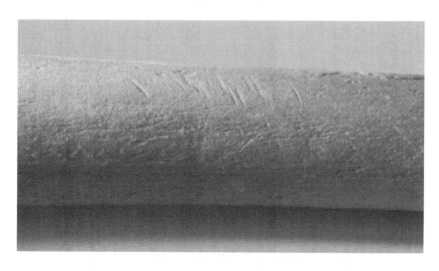

Above: Bone of a sacrificial victim of the Maya, showing butcher marks where the meat was cut off the bone with obsidian knives.

There is a Spanish eyewitness to the cannibalism that the Maya practiced. Jerónimo de Aguilar, one of the survivors of the 1511 shipwreck on the Quintana Roo coast, reported that the Maya sacrificed four other of his fellow survivors and ate them. Bernal Díaz de Castillo also reported that Cozumel Maya sacrificed ten of the eleven Taino Indians who shipwrecked on Cozumel after their canoe washed up during a storm.

In *Crónica de la Nueva España*, Francisco Cervantes de Salazar says that the Maya on Cozumel *"offered many things to the idols, making very grand and solemn sacrifices, not only of brute animals, but also of men and women, young boys, old men, young girls, and old women)."*

Early historian Peter Martyr wrote of the Indians of Cozumel: *"They immolated boys and girls to the cemís which are the idols that they venerate."* He went on saying: *"they ate the upper arms and thighs and the muscular part of the calf."*

Above: Dining on the leftovers. From Fray Bernardino Sahagún's Historia general de las cosas de Nueva España, *1540-1585*

The charred bones of children found by archaeologist Anda attest to this macabre Maya version of BBQ. We know that the sacrifices of children and babies were a very common kind of sacrifice in Yucatán. Anda says of 2,500 bones taken from the sacred cenote of Chichen Itzá, seventy-nine percent were children who were between three and eleven years of age when they were killed. In 2010, archeologist Steven Houston of Brown University found a Maya tomb of a *halach uinic* with the remains of six children who had been sacrificed and buried with him. The children were all under two years of age. Next to the chieftain was a bowl with the charred skeletal remains of a baby. Another funeral of a Maya chieftain in Northern Belize had the remains of five slaughtered children, ranging from newly-born to eight-years-of-age.

Above: A scene from a Maya vessel, illustrating a small child being sacrificed from Justin Kerr's __The Maya Vase Book__.

Bernal Díaz del Castillo speaks of religious pilgrimages and sacrifices in Cozumel in his 1568 book, _La Historia Verdadera de la Conquista de Nueva España_. He wrote: *"There were some idols with very deformed features in Cozumel and they were in a shrine that they customarily used in that time and place to slaughter."* Cogolludo wrote: *"they arrived in Cozumel in completion of their promises, for the offering of their sacrifices."*

Above: A scene painted on a ceramic vessel depicting a Maya sacrifice, from Justin Kerr's The Maya Vase Book.

Another kind of sacrifice was one in which a person would practice self-mutilation as a way to appease the gods. Stingray spines were used by the men to pierce their penises and the blood was then dripped onto bark paper. Later, the paper was burned as an offering. Both men and women would also pierce their tongues with these sharp spines to offer the pain and blood to the gods.

Above: Image from the Codex Telleriano-Remensis illustrating how they pierced their tongues to offer blood to the gods.

The Maya also believed they were not the first men to inhabit the earth. They thought there were at least two previous races of men (one made of mud and another made of corn) who lived on earth before them and who were wiped out by great floods when they displeased the gods.

Maya postclassic culture

Shortly after a child was born to elite parents, they bound his head between a pair of wooden boards in order to deform the shape of his skull as it grew. The belief was an elongated head, with a high, sloping forehead was beautiful, whereas a round head was the sign of the lower classes. Crossed eyes were also considered beautiful, and to ensure a child's eyes crossed, the parents would suspend a small bead on a string between the infant's eyes so that he would constantly focus on the bead and pull the eye muscles inward. Noses, ears, and lips were pierced in both males and females at an early age, and stretched by the insertion of clay, jade, or obsidian discs. The Maya also liked to file their teeth into elaborate shapes and inlay pieces of jade, pyrite, or turquoise into them. Young men painted themselves all black until they were married. Later in life, many Maya acquired tattoos, often covering their face as well as other parts of the body. Scarification was also practiced.

The women normally wore a long, loose, cotton blouse, similar to a *huipile*. Their hair was worn long, either in braids or parted down the middle. The men wore a strip of cotton cloth wrapped around their loins like a diaper and sometimes a large, square cotton cape over their shoulders. Both men and women wore sandals and an assortment of necklaces, bracelets, wrist-cuffs, ankle bracelets, and armbands. Members of the ruling class were the only ones with the authority to wear feathers and they did so by having them made into headdresses, capes, and hats. They also wore jaguar skin capes at times and ostentatious displays of jade.

The Tulum Maya had a wide-ranging diet. Fish and shellfish were one of the main ingredients, but they also ate the meat of the birds and animals they hunted (deer, peccary, monkeys, iguana, turtles, manatees, *tepezcuintle* or paca, rabbit, armadillo, and crocodile) as well as the flesh of their domesticated doves and turkeys. Besides raising fowl, they also bred a type of small dog, called the *techichi*, or *tzom* for consumption. In 1567 it was reported that they *"ate these dogs as the Spanish do rabbits. Those intended for this purpose were castrated in order to fatten them."* Their fields provided manioc (a tuber), corn, squash, black beans, chilies, bananas, pineapples, and greens, while the forest provided ramon (Maya breadfruit tree), fruits, cacao, and nuts. They loved honey and were avid bee-keepers, raising the Yucatán's stingless-bee in hollow logs.

Above: A Mayan codex.

The Maya developed a written language and with it they recorded their history, religious practices, astronomical observations, and much more in books made of *amatl*-bark covered in gesso (plaster). These books were around 8 inches high and as much as 11 feet long and folded up in accordion folds. Unfortunately, zealous Spanish priests, led by Bishop Diego de Landa, gathered up and burned all but three of these books in the 1500s. Apart from these three works (called codices) and a fragment of a fourth, the only other examples of Mayan writing left are the inscriptions in stone (on temples and monuments called stelae), ceramics (jars and plates), and pieces of carved jade, bone, and shell ornaments.

The Mayan system of writing is only now beginning to be deciphered. It is a logosyllabic system, in which the symbols (the glyphs or graphemes) can represent either a phoneme or an idea, similar to the Japanese written language. Although these glyphs were somewhat standardized, they were often drawn very differently by different scribes in different areas and times, leading to more confusion for today's code-breakers who are working on their decipherment. Around 300 of the 500 or so glyphs in the Mayan language represented a single word, or idea. The other 200 had a syllabic interpretation and were used as phonemes. When a glyph was used to represent the sound of a syllable, it was conjoined with other glyphs that also worked as phonemes and they were read all together as one word. The manner in which these phoneme glyphs were grouped together as one compound glyph was not standardized, but instead left to the scribe's own sense of artistry. Sometimes a phoneme glyph was incorporated into another glyph in the compound glyph as a piece of adornment, or it may simply be drawn directly to the side, top, or bottom of the other. Sometimes only parts of glyphs were used, similar to our use of contractions today.

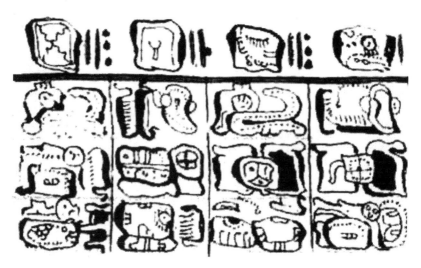

Above: Mayan hieroglyphics.

Above: Yuri Knorokov, the Russian linguist who figured out the secret to deciphering Mayan glyphs, although he wasn't given credit for it until much later.

The Maya developed a system of mathematics as well. With this system, they were able to compute the orbits of stars, moons, and the planets Venus, Mars, Mercury, and Jupiter. Using calculations based on the earth's rotation around the sun, they were able to keep a calendar that was extremely accurate. This calendar was originally designed by the Olmec and later adapted by the Maya. The Maya numbering system was vigesimal, that is, it had a base of twenty unlike our system based on ten. A round dot signified one, two dots two, and so on to five, which was a solid bar. Zero was indicated by a shell-shaped glyph. Unlike our system, which records numbers from left to right in order of rank (thousands, hundreds, tens, ones), the Maya recorded their numbers vertically, with the highest number on the bottom (three dots side by side over a bar over a bar would be 13, or 5+5+1+1+1). To indicate numbers higher than 19, a dot would be placed over the number to add 20 to the number.

Above: The Mayan number 13.

The Maya also dabbled in psychoactive drugs. For example they often employed the poisonous secretions of the *Buffo marinus* toad to fall into a hallucinatory trance powered by the bufotenin in the secretion. The 17th century friar, Thomas Gage, wrote that the Maya often "steeped" *Bufo* toads in bowls of *chicha* or *balché* (fermented ritual drinks) in order to give it extra potency and this use was also responsible for the inadvertent deaths of many of the imbibers of the toad-enhanced *chicha*. The toad-laced *chicha* must not have tasted very good, since it was often taken as an enema.

Above: Ancient Maya figurine depicting a toad-laced chicha enema.

The Maya also used a relative of the Morning Glory called the Xtabentun vine (*Turbina corymbosa*) to get high. The nectar of the flower of this vine is highly charged with the alkaloid ergine (LSA, or Lysergic Acid Amide) and when the stingless Yucatán bee uses this nectar to make its honey, the psychoactive ingredient is passed intact to the honey. The Maya found that sweetening their *chicha* or *balché* with this honey would enhance its inebriating effects.

The Maya connection to Phoenicia, Atlantis, Israel and India

The oft–quoted archaeologist Eric Thompson called the Putún Maya sea-traders the "Phoenicians of the New World," but he did not mean they had actually come from ancient Phoenicia; he was using the term as a metaphor. However, a handful of crack-pots have tried to prove that the Maya civilization was actually founded by the Phoenicians. What do they use for evidence of this incredible connection? Some pretty flimsy assertions, like the one put forward in the book Why and How the Ice Age Ended & The True History of the Pontic (White) Race: *"The name Maya is the same as the Phoenician goddess Maya. The pyramids and all the civilization signs are at about the same parallel with where the Phoenicians were. All celestial knowledge the Maya had was well known to have belonged to the Phoenicians."* In the book <u>The Crystal Skulls: Astonishing Portals to Man's Past</u>, the facts that the Phoenicians and the Maya both used purple dye was supposedly reason enough to prove the two civilizations were linked. The point that the Maya got their purple dye from the cochineal insect and dyewood and the Phoenicians got theirs from sea snails was deemed irreverent by the author of that book.

Another hare-brained notion that a few people actually believe is that the Maya civilization was founded by seafaring Tamils from India. Part of "proof" cited to support this theory is that both cultures worshiped "long nosed" gods; the Tamil worshiped the elephant god Ganesha and the Maya prayed to their long-nosed rain god, Chaac. The rest of their evidence is even weaker: Both cultures had brown skin; The word "Maya" appears in both the Tamil and Mayan languages; Both cultures were seasoned seafarers, and; Both cultures built stone temples. One crazy author even asserts the name Tamil is where the word "tamale" comes from!

Above left: the Maya god Chaac.   Above right: the Hindu god Ganesha

The misguided authors of these aforementioned books and articles were, unfortunately, not alone in trying to prove that the origins of the Maya civilization lay somewhere outside of the Americas. Some people, like Augustus Leplongeon, tried to prove the Maya actually originated in Atlantis.

Above: Agustus Leplongeon

Augustus Leplongeon was a British Freemason and amateur archaeologist who traveled throughout Yucatán in the 1870s and 1880s, excavating

Maya ruins and photographing Maya sites along the way. He made extensive excavations in Chichen Itzá in 1876, where he and his wife, Alice Dixon Leplongeon, uncovered the famous Toltec-style "Chac Mool," a statue of a reclining god holding a plate on his stomach. He tried to export this statue to the United States, but the director of the museum in Merida, Juan Peón Contreras de Elizalde, managed to stop the removal of the statue and kept it in Mexico. Later, this same museum director began to suffer delusions that he was the Messiah and travelled to Tulum to reign over the Maya there, as you will read about later in this book.

Above: Augustus Leplongeon with his Chac Mool at Chichen Itzá.

Together, Alice and Augustus claimed to have "deciphered" the Maya manuscript known as the Madrid Codex (a.k.a. the Tro-Cortesianus Codex or the Troano Codex), long before the key to the Maya hieroglyphic text was unlocked. In reality, what the pair did was make up an intricate story out of thin air, which described the life and love of "Queen Mu" and the "Prince Chacmol." Although the story was a complete fabrication based on nothing else but fertile imaginations, the name the Leplongeon's gave to the statue (Chac Mool) stuck, and has been used by archaeologists and laymen alike to describe the Leplongeon's find, as well as similar statues discovered in subsequent years. The Leplongeon's asserted link between the Maya and Atlantis, however, has been thoroughly debunked.

Other arm-chair ethnographers have claimed that the Maya were actually "the lost tribe of Israel," wandering Jews who had made their way to the New World centuries before Columbus. This view was seriously espoused by Edward King, or "the Viscount and third Lord of Kingsborough, Baron of Kingston, and Governor of the County of Cork," as he was better known in England. Lord Kingsborough had run across an Aztec codex in the Bodleian library at Oxford in 1814 and became obsessed with determining the origins of the various Mexican cultures. Between 1830 and 1848, Kingsborough published nine volumes of his work, Antiquities of Mexico. In volume 6, he wrote a 200 pages essay entitled "Arguments to Show that the Jews in Early Ages Colonized America."

Two of the arguments Kingsborough made to bolster his claim that the Maya were descendants of the "wandering tribes of Israel" were the "hooked noses" depicted on Maya carvings at Palenque and the fact that both the early Jews and the early Maya performed animal sacrifices. If that isn't enough to convince you, I cannot imagine what will.

Earlier authors had also tried to make this connection between the Jews and the Maya. Gonzalo Fernandez de Oviedo y Valdes, the Historiador de las Indias, and Italian-born historian Peter Martyr d'Anghiera, both wrote that the New World Indians performed the Jewish ritual of male circumcision. This little misunderstanding had its roots in the garbled reports that the early Spanish explorers made which were efforts to describe the blood-letting sacrifices the ancient Mexicans practiced. The Maya men would often pierce their foreskins with stingray spines, agave thorns, or obsidian blades, which produced a tattered foreskin. This damage was not the goal, but just the result of the blood-letting and there was obviously no connection between this practice and the Jewish practice of circumcision.

The Spanish arrive in Yucatán

After Cristóbal Colón returned to Spain at the end of his fourth voyage, he was a broken and dishonored man. In the Spanish Crown's eyes, he had failed miserably to find a way to Cathay, to establish any viable colonies in the newly discovered lands, or even to find any sources of the small amounts of gold he brought back to Spain. To add insult to injury, when he lost all four of his ships on his last voyage to the wood boring *teredo* worms, he had to pay for a ride back to Spain from Cuba on another ship. The Spanish King stripped Colón of his rights to govern the lands he had discovered during his four voyages and gave that authority to several other people in the Admiral's stead. Two of these new governors were Alonso de Hojeda and Diego de Nicuesa.

Diego de Nicuesa had traveled with Colón on his second and third voyages and had come to know many of the islands in the Caribbean, but he had not been with Colón when the old explorer had discovered the coast of Panamá on his fourth and last voyage. It may have been a surprise to Nicuesa then, when in 1508, King Ferdinand awarded him with the right to govern a land he had never seen. At the same time that Nicuesa was given his new fiefdom, King Ferdinand also gave Alonso de Hojeda the right to govern a contiguous part of the Panamanian and Colombian coast farther to the east. The two men began recruiting colonists, soldiers, and seamen (some of whom also had been on some of Colón's previous voyages) to make the journey to the new lands. Once fully staffed, they agreed to have their fleets meet up in the Bay of Cartagena, Colombia, and go their separate ways from there. Nicuesa's fleet of twelve ships left shortly after Hojeda's in 1509 with seven hundred and eighty-five men and one pregnant mare.

The two fleets met as planned in Colombia, and then parted ways. Nicuesa stumbled along the coast of Panama almost to Costa Rica, losing several of his ships and most of his men to starvation and hostile Indian attacks along the way. He finally turned back, arriving in Hojeda's camp months later, with only 60 of his original 785 expedition members left alive. They had eaten the mare.

Nicuesa found that Hojeda had been replaced by Vasco Núñez de Balboa. Not happy with finding himself saddled with sixty hungry, weak men, Balboa decided to ship them back to Hispaniola. The leaky caravel the men had sailed from Panama was pressed into service for this task.

By now the gold had piled up at the new colony in an amount that was enough to warrant sending the King his share, the *Quinto Real* or Royal Fifth. Balboa wrote a letter to the governor of Hispaniola, Diego Colón, requesting the gold he was sending be forwarded to the King in Spain. He also sent back a large group of Indian slaves they had captured and appended a long list of supplies he would like Colón to send the colony in return for them. He chose Juan de Valdivia to captain the ship carrying the gold, slaves, and letters. Valdivia, in turn, chose a hardy fellow who was one of the sixty survivors of the Nicuesa expedition to go along on the voyage. That man was later to become known as Gonzalo Guerrero.

Unfortunately, the ship carrying Valdivia and his crew never made it to Hispaniola. It hit a reef during a storm just south of Jamaica and sank, with all but twenty of the Spaniards drowning during the wrecking event. While these twenty survivors drifted in a salvaged longboat, eight more died of dehydration. Their bodies were eaten by their fellow crewmembers. The remaining twelve of the shipwreck survivors came to shore two weeks later on the Quintana Roo coast, where they were found and taken captive by the Maya. There, five of the Spaniards, including Valdivia, were sacrificed to the gods, after which their bodies were roasted and eaten. Seeing their fate, the seven remaining Spaniards managed to escape, including "Gonzalo" and a deacon named Jerónimo de Aguilar. Their freedom did not last long, however, and they were taken captive once more, this time by a different group of Maya. The seven were taken to Xamanzamá (present day Tancah) a village located just to the north of Tulum. One by one the Spaniards began to die from overwork and abuse. After a couple of years, only "Gonzalo" and Jerónimo were left alive.

In 1517, Francisco Hernández de Córdoba sailed from the island of Fernandina (present-day Cuba) on what he said was a slaving expedition to neighboring Caribbean islands, but later he claimed that he was caught in a storm in the Yucatán Channel and blown off-course. Actually, this claim of "accidentally" finding a new land was invented to avoid getting in hot water with the King of Spain, who had just issued a decree halting further exploration of the New World for the time being. In truth, that had been the plan all along. Córdoba had enlisted the services of Antón de Alaminos, the ship's pilot and navigator who had led Cristobal Colon through the waters off Honduras earlier. Surely, Alaminos had a good idea that there was new land to be found north of Honduras.

Cordoba later reported that "when the storm subsided," he found his fleet near the shore of a small, deserted island, which he named Isla Mujeres. His report says they named it that because of the many female idols they found in the abandoned temples there. Moving on to the mainland, at a place they named Cabo Catoche the Spaniards finally encountered a group of Maya, but through a lack of communication, each group began to feel threatened by the other and a fight ensued. Fifteen Spaniards were hurt (two of whom died a few days later) and over a dozen Maya killed in the confrontation. Two Spaniards were taken prisoner by the Maya and two Maya were taken prisoner by Córdoba's men. The two Spaniards later died as slaves, while the two Maya prisoners were baptized with the Christian names of Julián and Melchor and taken to Cuba. Later, the two served as translators for subsequent Spanish expeditions to the Yucatán. It was from these two Maya translators that the Spanish learned of the existence of the two Spanish castaways from the Valdivia shipwreck, Jerónimo and Gonzalo.

Above: Cordoba found the Maya on the mainland hostile.

In 1518, another Spanish expedition of 4 ships carrying 240 men departed Cuba for the Yucatán, this one led by Juan de Grijalva and carrying Julián and Melchor aboard as translators. They made the crossing in two days, arriving in Cozumel on May 3. Juan Díaz Núñez, the expedition's chaplain, later wrote *"We beheld a new land and approaching it we saw on a certain headland a stone house and huts and since the well-known discovery on the cross was on that day we gave the island the name of Santa Cruz de Puerta Latina."* Díaz went on to write *"we saw the place was full of sandbanks and reefs, so we went close to the other side where we saw the white house more clearly. It was a small tower which seemed to be long as a house and as tall as a man."* Grijalva anchored his ships near present-day town of San Miguel, and went ashore with the chaplain, the interpreters, and several soldiers. Díaz wrote that the town *"had stone houses with straw roofs, some modern and lately built and others which showed antiquity, very beautiful in appearance."* They found all the residents had fled into the jungle, except for an old man who was tending his cornfield. Julián and Melchor told him to go bring the people back, but he did not return, so Grijalva had the expedition's chaplain say mass on the steps of the largest temple, possibly near where the military air base now stands. Díaz said *"then the Indian who served as their priest came back and in his company were eight Indians who brought chickens of the land, honey, and certain roots they call maiz. The Captain said he only wanted gold... and gave them to understand that in exchange for it he would give them such merchandise as he brought with him for that purpose. These Indians took the Captain and some ten or twelve others and gave them a dinner in a hall, all surrounded by stone and covered with straw. In front of this was a well where all the people drank."*

The Spaniards stayed on Cozumel until May 7th, but just as they were preparing to leave, a woman ran up to them speaking in a dialect of the Cuban Indians, a language that a few of the Spaniards could understand. She told them she was from Jamaica. She recounted how she arrived on the island two years prior when she and her ten companions had their canoe caught up in the current and wash up on the east side of the island. They had been taken prisoner and the Maya sacrificed all but her. Grijalva took the Jamaican woman with him when they left Cozumel, and she became another one of the Spaniards translators.

Grijalva left Cozumel sailing south along the Quintana Roo coast, where he and his men sighted the Castillo at Tulum. Juan Díaz, expedition chaplain for Juan de Grijalva, described Tulum when he wrote: *"Near sunset we saw far off a town* [Tulum] *so large that the city of Seville seems no larger or better. In it a very large tower was visible. Many Indians ran along the shore with banners which they raised and lowered, signaling us to approach them, but the captain* [Juan de Grijalva] *was not willing."* Little did they know, Jerónimo de Aguilar, who had been shipwrecked 7 years earlier, was probably within sight of their ships as they sailed past.

Cozumel was the first stop Hernán Cortés made on his 1519 expedition to Mexico. The fleet of eleven ships finally arrived on Cozumel near Xamancab, today's San Miguel. Cortés sent his translators, Melchor and the Jamaican slave (now nick-named "La Jamaiquina") to find the chief of Cozumel and invite him to come and talk. The Maya leader consulted with his priests and they all agreed that Cortés arrival had been prophesied. They believed that he was sent by the gods to castigate them for their transgressions, so they surrendered their fate to his will. Using the power vested in him by the Maya prophesy, Cortés destroyed the Maya idols and erected a cross on top of their main temple. Bernal Díaz del Castillo, a member of the expedition, later wrote *"within the shrine were some little wooden chests. In these were other idols and some small medallions of half gold, mostly copper, some pendants, and three diadems."* He went on: *"at that moment there sallied from another house, which was an oratory of their idols, ten Indians clad in long, white, cotton cloaks, reaching to their feet, and with their long hair matted together, that it could never be parted or even combed again unless it were cut. These were the priests of the idols."*

During conversations with the *halach uinik*, Cortés got news about the status of the shipwrecked Spaniards, Gonzalo and Jerónimo. It had been eight years since the two had first been captured by the Maya. Cortés sent a messenger with a letter inviting the two to come to Cozumel and join his expedition and also gave the messenger quantities of green-glass beads to serve as payment to secure the release of the men if they were being held against their will. The messenger reached Jerónimo first and he was delighted at the chance to return to the company of his countrymen. As an ordained *diácono*, Jerónimo had endured the years in celibacy as a slave to the *batab* of Xamanzamá. While prisoner he kept his Book of Hours (a religious book of prayer schedules) and in it, a running count of the days since his capture. His count was only three days off at the time of his release.

Aguilar jumped at the chance to return to Spain. With the beads he bought his freedom, but as it turned out, Aguilar never informed his fellow castaway of the arrival of the letter and beads because Gonzalo lived too far away in Chetumal to get word to him before Cortez sailed.

When Jerónimo turned over the glass beads to his owner, he was given his freedom and he rushed to Cozumel. Unfortunately, he took too long to make the trip to the island and was the first foreigner in Cozumel to "miss the boat," Cortés having sailed on without him the day before. Bitterly disappointed at being too late, he was later delighted when the ships returned to Cozumel the next day for emergency repairs. Cortés welcomed him and they all left together four days later, sailing north to eventually land at Veracruz and march inland to Tenochtitlan where Cortés would capture Moctezuma and defeat the Aztec empire. Jerónimo told Cortés that Guerrero refused to come and chose instead to stay with his adopted people; hiding the fact that he never sent word to his fellow castaway about the opportunity to be rescued. Gonzalo eventually died, never rejoining the rest of the Spaniards.

Today, there are statues, murals, poems, and popular books dedicated to telling the story of this Gonzalo, but most of the story is based on fiction. The legend most people are familiar with is that after he was shipwrecked in Yucatán in 1511, he was enslaved by the Maya. Gonzalo was supposed to have worked his way up from this lowly position to the second highest in the land, that of *nacom*, or war chief, second only to the *batab*, or high chief of the Maya town of Ichpaatún. And, as in all good fairytales, our hero supposedly married a Maya princess. The legend also says when Gonzalo was approached by fellow shipwreck survivor Jerónimo Aguilar with a letter that Hernán Cortés had sent from Cozumel in 1519, offering to rescue them, he refused the offer and chose instead to stay with his family and fight against his former countrymen. Later, he was supposedly killed by a Spaniard in a battle in Honduras.

But what is the truth? What are the sources for this incredible story?

First, it is important to know that the name "Gonzalo Guerrero" never appeared in any written document until Francisco López de Gomara published his *Histora General de las Indias* in 1552. The first mention of the shipwreck survivors was in the orders from the Governor of Cuba that Hernán Cortés had with him when he set off on his expedition in 1519. When Julián and Melchor, the two Maya who Francisco Hernández de Córdoba had captured in 1517 were taken to Cuba in that year, they told the Spanish of the castaways' existence and that the men were being held by the Maya as slaves. Cortés was ordered by Cuban Governor

Diego de Velázquez to sail by the coast of *"Yucatán Santa María de los Remedios where there were some Christians being held by caciques who Melchor knows."*

The second mention of "Gonzalo" was likewise not by name, but by inference only, in a letter Hernán Cortés sent to Spain dated July 10, 1519. In the letter, Cortés seems to refute the much later story put forth by others that "Gonzalo" refused to be rescued and instead he says it simply was not convenient for the expedition to waste much time in a search for the shipwrecked sailor. The letter states, in part: *"By this Jerónimo de Aguilar we were informed that there were other Spaniards in that caravel that sank and that they were spread out far and wide across the land, which, he informed us, was very large and it was impossible for us to be able to gather them up without wasting a lot of time."*

Andrés de Tapia, the Spaniard who first talked to Aguilar on Cozumel in 1519, stated in his 1539 account of the meeting that the shipwreck survivor had told him *"the other Spaniard had taken an Indian woman as a wife, and the Indians had killed all the other Spaniards; and he thought that other one, his companion, did not want to come because other times he had talked to him he said he had pierced his ears and nose and tattooed his face and hands, and for that reason he didn't ask him when they came."* Again, it seems that "Gonzalo" was never actually asked by Aguilar if he wanted to be rescued or not.

Cortés did not write again about "Gonzalo" until 1534, in an interrogatory he submitted during a court case. In the document, Cortés states he was told by Jerónimo de Aguilar *"that many of the shipwrecked sailors who survived the wrecking event later died, and only eight or nine made it to Yucatán, but in very poor condition... and if it hadn't been for the Indians capturing them, they would have all died. Regardless, all except two died anyway."* These two survivors, Cortés wrote *"...were one Jerónimo de Aguilar and the other one a **Morales**, who did not want to come because he had pierced his ears, was painted [tattooed] like an Indian, had married an Indian, and had children with her."* Francisco Cervantes de

Salazar, a good friend and confidant of Cortés, also refers to the second shipwreck survivor as *"Fulano* [guy; fellow] *de Morales"* in his recounting of the tale in his *Crónica de la Nueva España,* published in 1558.

In 1536, a letter from the *Contador de Honduras-Higueras,* Andrés de Cerezada, tells of finding the body of a Spaniard who died on the battlefield in 1534 in the Uluá River valley, but he too gives the man a name other than Gonzalo Guerrero: *"the Spanish Christian,* **Gonzalo Aroça***, who had been with the Indians in Yucatán twenty years now died by an arquebus shot."* The original of this letter says nothing of how the man was dressed or how his body looked; the description of a Spaniard *"almost naked, dressed like an Indian and tattooed"* came from an invented description that appeared in Robert Chamberlain's 1948 book, The Conquest and Colonization of Yucatán.

When Gonzalo Fernández Oviedo y Valdés published his *Historia general y natural de las Indias* in 1535, he avoided the thorny problem of Gonzalo's last name entirely, by simply calling him *"Gonzalo, a sailor."* Regardless, Oviedo decided to embellish the story by adding many details that had not been recorded previously by anyone else. It was in this book that the legend of "Gonzalo Guerrero" was born. He was a *"son of a Hidalgo,"* wrote Oviedo, and went on to say that Francisco Montejo the *Adelantado* had sent Gonzalo a letter in 1527, offering to make him the highest ranking Spaniard in Yucatán, if he would only leave the Indians and join the Spanish. Gonzalo was supposed to had replied by means of a note written on the back of the letter, which Oviedo quotes: *"Sir, I kiss your Excellency's hand, but as I am a slave, I am not free, even though I am married and have a wife and children, I believe in God and you and the Spanish can always count on my friendship."*

Using this embellished story of Oviedo's as a starting point, Francisco López de Gomara wrote about Gonzalo in his 1552 *Historia General de las Indias y conquista de Mexico,* adding many more details about the man and solidifying the mythological image of Gonzalo as a warrior. Gomara also attached the last name of **Guerrero** to him for the first time, eschewing either **Morales** or **Aroça**, the names he was identified by in earlier records (although Gomara also referred to him twice as Gonzalo **Herrero,** earlier in his writings). Gomara wrote (33 years after the fact) that *"Gonzalo **Herrero**, sailor, was with Nachanchán, the lord of Chectemal, and he married a rich lady of that town, and he had children, and he was the war captain of Nachanchán, and was held in high esteem for the victories he had during the wars with neighboring kingdoms."* Gómara also combined Tapia's description of Gonzalo with that of Cortés', adding that it was either for the shame of the way he now looked or the shame of being married to an Indian or the love of his children that he refused to rejoin the Spanish. In addition, many more elements were added to the story that had never appeared before, such as the entire, word-for-word text of the letter Cortés wrote to Aguilar, the idea that the letter was hidden in the hair of the messenger, and the word-for-word recital of the conversation between Aguilar and Andrés de Tapia in Cozumel.

Fray Diego de Landa added more details to the story in his 1566 manuscript *Relación de cosas de Yucatán*, and repeated Cortés and Tapia's statements that Aguilar was never able to go and see Gonzalo, as he was living too far away. He also repeated Oviedo's statement that Gonzalo was a war captain in Chectemal (Chetumal), married a woman there, had children, pierced his ears, and added the new bit that Gonzalo taught the Maya the Spanish style of warfare.

In the late 1560s, Bernal Díaz del Castillo wrote his *Historia Verdadera de la Conquista de la Nueva España,* in which he actually <u>quoted</u> (supposedly from memory, even though he wasn't present at the time) what Gonzalo was to have said to Aguilar in 1519, over 45 years earlier. The fabricated conversation reads: *"Brother Aguilar, I am married, I have three children, they have made me war captain in time of war; you go with God's blessing, I have my face tattooed and my ears pierced. What would they think of me if the Spanish saw me like this? And I have my beautiful children. For their sake, leave me these green beads that you bring, and I will give them to my children, and tell them my brothers sent them from my land."* At this, Díaz del Castillo says Gonzalo's wife interrupted and sent Aguilar away. This story, copied from Díaz del Castillo's work, was repeated in Diego López de Cogolludo's 1688 book, *Historia de Yucatán*. Antonio de Solis y Ribadeneyra piled on more fabrication in his 1684 book *Historia de la conquista de México*, raising the number of Gonzalo's children to *"three or four,"* and attributing the real reason for him refusing to join Cortés was his love for his Indian wife.

In 1974, Mario Aguirre Rosas, a writer for the Mexico City newspaper *El Universal*, published what he described as Gonzalo Guerrero's diary, supposedly written on deerskin velum and sheets of 16th century European paper. However, no one except Aguirre was able to examine the original manuscript, which Aguirre said belonged to a private collector named José López Pérez who would let no one else see it. This purported autobiography of Gonzalo, parts of which Aguirre later published in his newspaper, was full of fabricated details, which have been repeated *ad nauseam* by uninformed, amateur historians who read the mendacious tale and believed it to be authentic. It is in this fairy-tale invented by Aguirre that the myth Gonzalo's wife was a princess named Zazil first started, as well as many other details about the man that are patently false. In 1975, two thousand copies of *Gonzalo de Guerrero: Padre del mestizaje iberoamericano* by Aguirre were printed in Mexico City by Editorial Jus. The book was simply a rehash of his newspaper articles about his spurious autobiographical document of Gonzalo Guerrero.

Much later, in 1994, a mysterious manuscript appeared in Mexico City that was claimed to be written by Fray San Buenaventura of Mérida in 1724, purportedly describing a manuscript in the priest's possession written partially on paper and partially on deerskin by none other than Gonzalo Guerrero, in which he tells the story of his life. The Buenaventura document has been discredited; an invention connected to Aguirre's work and made in order to deceive. It was written on paper of a later manufacture and containing many passages copied from earlier historical works, but it was published nevertheless in 1994 as *Historias de la conquista del Mayab, 1511-1697 de Fray Joseph de San Buenaventura* by the Universidad Autónoma de Yucatán.

So, just what do we know for certain about Gonzalo, the shipwrecked Spaniard? We know that he was in Panamá with Diego de Nicuesa and later with Nuñez de Balboa, when he was sent on a fateful voyage that ended abruptly off the shores of Jamaica, resulting in him being cast-away on the coast of Yucatán. We know that he lived the rest of his life with the Maya, married, had children, and acquired some kind of body modification as adornment. But, that is it; that is all we know for sure. All other details above and beyond these scant facts are fabrications. We do not even know his real name.

Zamá, the original name of Tulum

Tulum (meaning "rampart" or "wall" in Mayan) is the name now given to the ruined Maya city that the pre-Hispanic and Colonial Period Maya knew prior to its abandonment as Zamá, from the Mayan word meaning "tomorrow." Zamal, in Mayan, means "dawn" or "daybreak." The name Zamá is often translated incorrectly as "the city of dawn," which is only an English nick-name that archaeologist Samuel Lothrop first bestowed on the city in 1922. The original name of Zamá is thought to come from the fact that the city was closely associated with both the East, the direction of the new day.

The Maya of pre-Conquest Tulum lived all along a long swath of coast, bordered by the site now known as Tancah in the north and the spread of ceremonial buildings and residences just south of today's Tulum to the south. The whole area was under the rule of one royal house. Initially, in the Late Postclassic, the main ceremonial and population center for this "mini metropolis" was in Tancah; the walled ceremonial center of Tulum had not yet been built. Later, around 1200 A.D., the ceremonial center we now call Tulum was built and the old center of Tancah (which was then called Xamanzama, or "north Zamá") began to decline.

By the time of the arrival of the Spanish, Xamanzama/Tancah was the smaller of the two "downtowns," and Zamá/Tulum was the larger. The Spanish, however, did not really distinguish between the two, and often called the entire "mini metropolis" Zamá, Tzamá, or Çamá.

Beginning in 1527, from his base of operation at Xel Ha (later he moved it to the coast of Tabasco) the Spanish conquistador Francisco Montejo *(el Adelantado)* waged a war against the Maya of the Yucatán and by 1547, he and his son and nephew had the entire peninsula under their control. Maya villages were handed out to their fellow conquistadors as rewards for their participation in the battles, and the Maya living on these feudal lands, or *encomiendas,* were often moved to other places more convenient to the Spaniards. This forced resettlement, along with a massive decline in the Maya population due to European diseases brought to the New World by the Spanish, is most likely what decimated the Maya of Tulum/Tancah by the end of the 1500s. To get a picture of how devastating these Old World diseases were to the New World Indians, of the estimated 10,000 Maya who were living on Cozumel when it was discovered by Grijalva in 1518, there were only 186 men and 172 women left in 1570, only 52 years later.

The first European mention of the Zamá place-name was in 1549 when a census was taken there. It reported only 88 tribute-paying men, or around 350 people in total. In 1570, a letter from Yucatán's Bishop Francisco de Toral was addressed to the people of *"Cozumel, Ppole, and Tzamá."* This is the only example of this alternate spelling (Tzamá) used in reference to the town. In other Colonial Period documents and censuses, Tzamá shows up as a Mayan surname, but oddly, no one was ever registered with that name in Tulum or Tancah. There were some families with that name in Cozumel, however. Ppole and Polé were both the pre-twentieth-century ways of spelling the name of the Maya site known today as Xcaret.

In 1579 a document written by Juan de Reigosa entitled *"Relación geográfica de Çamá,"* stated that Zamá was once *"a settlement of many Indians and during the past 20 years a large number have died,* [due to smallpox] *so that today* [1579] *in the town there are fewer than 50 tribute-paying Indians, who are poor in spirit and without energy."* Reigosa also stated in the document that *"in the language of the Indians, Zama means tomorrow."* He also mentions in his report that canoes would come to Tulum from Honduras and that when they were out in the open sea they would use the structure known as "El Castillo" as a landmark, which they called *la mesa de Zamá.*"

A 1665 Spanish document lists the governor of Zamá as Francisco Cauich. In a census of the combined towns of Zamá and Polé in 1668, there were only 25 adult male Maya living in those two towns. By the 1700s, Tulum and Tancah had been, for all practical purposes, abandoned. The city's ceremonial buildings fell into ruin and only the occasional passing Maya would stop by to offer a small sacrifice in the decaying rooms. The jungle eventually took back over, hiding the city beneath a heavy covering of vegetation.

Stephens and Catherwood, the Mormons, and Henry Wadsworth Longfellow

The ruins of Tulum lay hidden and unmolested in the jungle until 1841, when an American adventurer named John Lloyd Stephens and a British artist named Frederick Catherwood stayed at the ruins for over a week during their tour of Yucatán. Although the pair found the ruins covered in vines and trees, they also discovered signs of recent rituals and offerings left behind by the Maya in one of the buildings. Stephens later wrote a book about the trip, *Incidents of Travel in Yucatán*, and published it in 1843. Engravings of drawings made by Catherwood at Tulum were included in the book. It was a run-away best-seller.

In 1844, Frederick Catherwood published *Views of Ancient Monuments Central America, Chiapas and Yucatán*, which contained several lithographs of Tulum that he drew at the ruins in 1841 with the aid of a *camera lucida*.

A copy of Stephens very popular book was sent by a Mormon named John Bernhisel to the Latter Day Saint (LDS) Prophet Joseph Smith, who wrote a review of it. Mentions of this review appeared in the official LDS publication *Times and Seasons* in the September 15, and October 1 1842 volumes. In the publication, Smith wrote of Stephens' book: *"Of all the histories that have been written pertaining to the antiquities of this country it is the most correct, luminous and comprehensive, and it supports the testimony of the Book of Mormon."*

Above: The rendering of El Castillo done by Catherwood in 1841 that appeared in Stevens' book Incidents of Travel in Yucatán.

As Smith studied *Incidents of Travel in Yucatán* more and more, he began to read into it the proof he was looking for; namely that Jesus Christ (embodied as the postclassic Maya god **Kukulcan**) once lived in Yucatán. Smith spoke often of Stevens' book (and of his earlier book, *Incidents of Travel in Central America, Chiapas, and Yucatán*) to other LDS members, who also were captivated by it. In 1849, five years after Smith was killed by a mob as he awaited trial in a Carthage, Illinois jail on charges of riot and treason, LDS leader Orson Pratt wrote another review of the book in the *Millennial Star.* *"...the Book of Mormon gives us the names and locations of great numbers of cities in the very region where Catherwood and Stephens afterwards discovered them. The Book of Mormon says that in the 367th day after Christ, the Lamanites, the forefathers of the American Indians, took possession of the city of Desolation, which was in Central America, near to or in Yucatán... the Nephites being the nation* *who inhabited the cities of Yucatán."* The LDS church over the next century fielded several expeditions to Yucatán searching for ruins that would match *"The city Bountiful of the Book of Mormon,"* a site they described as *"...an important walled city and military center of the first century B. C. and the place of the resurrected Christ appeared to the surviving Nephites following the cataclysm incident to his crucifixion, a location of key importance in the Book of Mormon geography."*

The Mormons weren't the only folks fascinated by *Incidents of Travel in Yucatán.* In 1879 Henry Wadsworth Longfellow published the poem "Tuloom." The opening lines read:

> *"On the coast of Yucatán,*
> *as untenanted of man,*
> *as a castle under ban,*
> *by a doom*
> *for the deeds of bloody hours,*
> *overgrown with tropic bowers,*
> *stand the teocallis towers*
> *of Tuloom."*

I will spare you from the remaining 26 stanzas of the poem.

The Cult of the Talking Cross

In 1847, the Maya of the Yucatán revolted against the Spanish and mestizos who had taken control of the land that was formerly theirs. The Maya organized themselves into fighting units and began to raid haciendas and towns throughout the southern portion of the peninsula, killing and mutilating the bodies of any non-Maya they could catch. Pandemonium reigned. Over the next few years, the non-Maya were forced farther and farther northward, seemingly incapable of stopping the onslaught.

During this period of chaos, a new religious cult sprang up amongst the Maya rebel ranks; *el Culto de la Cruz Parlante* (the Cult of the Talking Cross). The members of this cult were called the *Cruzoob,* the Spanish word for "cross" pluralized by the Mayan suffix *oob*. The origins of the cult can be traced back to the Maya "talking idols," one of which had been located on Cozumel when the Spanish arrived in 1517. These were small, hollow idols holding the ashes of other dead chieftains. The Maya priests used a long, hollow wooden tube to speak through and simulate the voice of the god, while standing or crouching in the small sacristy behind these idols. Oviedo says in his book: *"outside of their towns they have a big shrine where they keep the tutelary cemí [idol]. There the cacique [chief] and priests gather, who hide behind the idol's back and spoke as if with its own voice whatever the cacique suggested to them. During the events when they celebrate, they brought food to the idol, and the priests availed themselves of the offerings."* Another early description of the process says: *"The Christians went inside the said house, and suddenly, the cemí [idol] shouted loudly and spoke in its language, but what we found was that it was an artifice: because it was hollow, a blowgun or tube could be fitted into its lower part and then stretched to a dark part of the house, covered with fronds, where there was a person who spoke whatever the cacique wanted it to say, by speaking through the blowgun. So our people, suspecting just what it could be, kicked the cemí and found what we just described. The cacique, seeing that we had exposed it, begged with great insistence that we not say a thing to the other Indians, his vassals, nor to others, because through that trick he kept all of them in obedience."*

The *Culto de la Cruz Parlante* began on October 15, 1850, when a mestizo named José María Barrera placed a small wooden cross on a platform next to a cenote outside the town; a town now known as Felipe Carrillo Puerto. Standing alongside, a Maya rebel ventriloquist named Manuel Nahuat would throw his voice, making it appear as if his words were coming from the cross. The cross (via Nahuat) told the rebels that they had suffered enough and now they had been singled out by God to be his chosen people. Many Maya rebels fell hard for the ruse and soon a new town was established around the cross, Xbalam Na Kampocolche Chan Santa Cruz. A new military theocracy formed within the rebel cross-worshipers as well, headed by the priests who interpreted the messages of the ventriloquist. Later, Barrera and Nahuat disappeared and were replaced by a high priest, Juan de la Cruz Puc, who presented God's wishes to the *Cruzoob* in written form. Soon, other centers of *Cruz Parlante* worship appeared, in villages like Muyil, Xpalma, Chumpón, San Antonio Muyil, and Tulum Pueblo, not far from the ruins.

In 1863 the headquarters of the Cruz Parlante Cruzoob was moved to Tulum Pueblo. In Tulum Pueblo, the high priestess of the cult (who was known as *La Santa Patrona*) was María Uicab, a charismatic and powerful woman who had left a string of husbands in her wake. By 1870, María had converted Tulum Pueblo into the center of the cult's operations, displacing Chan Santa Cruz as the most important rebel-held village in Yucatán. Sometime during her reign, a Spanish missionary came by boat to call on the priestess. She ordered him killed, the flesh removed from his skeleton, and his bones set in cement in the ruins of Tulum as a symbol of the power the *Cruz Parlante* had over the religions of the Spaniards. In the 1970s, I saw what remained of the priest's bones, which have since been removed.

Above: The bones of the Spanish priest were set in cement as a warning to others.

On January 21, 1871, a thousand government troops led by Coronel Daniel Traconis attacked Tulum Pueblo by surprise and captured María's son, forcing the High Priestess to flee for her life. Regrouping her troops, Maria counter-attacked on July 3, 1872. The counter attack was answered by the Mexican government troops almost immediately and from that time on, no word was ever heard from María, who was most likely killed in the battle.

Chan Santa Cruz was not happy in playing second fiddle to Tulum, and the *Cruzoob* leaders were always suspicious of their coastal competitor. The two centers continued to jockey for power during the 1870s and 1880s.

In 1887, the former director of the Merida Museum, Juan Peón Contreras de Elizalde (the younger brother of playwright and poet José Peón de Contreras) showed up on the beach at Tancah in a boat he had hired in Belize. Earlier that year, Juan had begun to tell people that he was the second Messiah. He started dressing in robes and carrying a cross around on his shoulder, telling everyone that he should now be called by his whole name, *"Juan the Baptist, the second Messiah, the Pilgrim, the True Confirmer."* Shortly thereafter, he resigned his post at the museum and hatched a plan to "bring peace to the Maya Rebels" and to make a killing in the logwood trade at the same time. Logwood (or dyewood) was the heartwood of a tree found in Yucatán that was used in making fabric dye and commanded a high price in the United States and Europe.

When Juan Peón landed in Tancah, he told the *Cruzoob* there that his name was "Juan Xiu" (a very Mayan name) and that he was the new "anointed one" of the *Cruz Parlante*. At first the Maya rebels of Tancah were suspicious of this audacious stranger, but soon they were on their knees, kissing the cross-emblazoned flag the man was carrying. Juan set up on the beach a pre-fabricated chapel that he had brought with him on his boat and then began to pass out gifts to the amazed *Cruzoob*.

His next move was to send gifts to the "High Priest" at Tulum, who came the next day with his entire entourage. The Tulum *Cruzoob* priest knelt before the stranger from Merida and said that his arrival had been prophesized by the talking cross, and indeed, he was to be the new top dog. After a three-day ceremony, in which the "Talking Cross" of Tulum reassured the *Cruzoob* that the man was indeed the prophicized one, he became known as the Second Messiah and conferred with the title "Governor of the Castillo and the Port of Tancah." Later, he was married to Isabel Xuluk, the widow of a deceased *Cruzoob* governor of Tulum, in an ornate ritual attended by *Cruzoob* leaders from Tulum, Tancah, and Muyil. The *Cruzoob* members of Chan Santa Cruz boycotted the event.

Above: Juan Peón Contreras de Elizalde and his disciple "Dorado" (Golden) who is cranking a hand organ.

Once he was "crowned," he put the *Cruzoob* to work cutting dyewood for him. When a satisfactory amount of the expensive wood had been cut and gathered, The Messiah had it all loaded on a ship which he boarded and sailed to Progreso, Yucatán, where he planned to sell the cargo. On the way, some of the *Cruzoob* who were traveling with him began to suspect that they had been hoodwinked and sent word back to Tulum about their discovery. When word reached the Maya rebel leaders, all hell broke loose. Furious that the *Cruzoob* of Tulum had been so gullible, the *Cruzoob* of Chan Santa Cruz, Muyil, and Chunpom attacked Tulum and Tancah and deposed their leaders.

That wasn't the end of the Tulum Maya rebels, though, not by a long shot. The war raged on for many more years, and the rebels eventually were left to rule their territory relatively undisturbed. The non-Maya knew the southern part of the peninsula was better left alone and rarely tried to enter *Cruzoob* land. However, one small group, tempted by the offer of cash, did make a landing at Tulum beach, with bloody results that ended up having an unexpected effect on the *Cruzoob* theocracy.

In the summer of 1897, a man reported to be a treasure hunter by the name of Dr. Juan Fábregas arrived on Cozumel with the intention of hiring a boat and crew to take him to Tulum. His request fell on deaf ears; as the War of the Casts was still in full swing and no one on Cozumel wanted to risk their lives by entering the mainland stronghold of the *Cruzoob* Maya rebels, or *Bravos* as they were called locally. But, money talks (in this case 13 pesos) and regardless of the danger, Fábregas eventually convinced Ruperto Loria to take him to Tulum.

Loria picked out a mate, 22-year-old Ignacio Novela, to help with the sailboat's rigging and at the last minute decided to take his 11-year-old stepson, Juan Bautista Vega, along for the ride. The trip across the channel was uneventful and the boat made landfall at Tulum beach safely. As the little group settled down for a quick lunch on the beach, they were approached by a group of Maya rebels from Tulum Pueblo. One thing lead to another, and soon Loria, Fábregas, and Novela were all killed. Young Juan Bautista Vega was hauled off to the village of Tulum and tied to a tree. There he remained for several days, unable to communicate with his captors, as he spoke no Mayan and they spoke no Spanish. Eventually, the boy was marched through Muyil and Chunpóm to Yokdzonot, where the *Cruzoob Gobernador*, Felipe Yama, ordered him to be executed. A black Belizean living with the rebels (known variously as Joe, José, Mr. Dyo, or Mr. Dio) pleaded for the boy's life, saying that the kid could be useful since he was able to read and write. Yama relented and Vega was allowed to live.

Vega stayed with Joe for the next several months while he learned Mayan, but was later turned over to the *Cruzoob* high priest of Chunpóm, Florentino Cituk, where he became the priest's secretary. The boy proved his worth translating messages between the *Cruzoob* and the Yucatán Army. He later married into Cituk's family and became thoroughly Maya, very similar to what happened to Gonzalo Guerrero almost 400 years earlier

.

Above: Juan Bautista Vega in 1962.

The *Cruzoob* rebels continued to fight engagements with the Mexican Army until a peace was negotiated in 1901. The treaty allowed the Maya to choose their own local government, but even so, many holdouts refused to honor the terms of the peace agreement and sporadic fighting continued to occur for nearly 20 more years. In 1915, after the death of Cituk, Vega was named high priest of the *Cruzoob* and became their maximum leader, bearing the rank of General in the *Cruzoob* military. In 1918, the final peace agreement was at last worked out and the War of the Casts was over. Although he visited Cozumel in 1926, Vega never returned to live on the island. He died on July 28, 1969, still the highest ranking *Cruzoob* official.

Above: General Paulino Caamal (right) the Tulum Cruzoob general who killed Juan Bautista Vegas stepfather in 1897. Photo taken in 1926 as Caamal and Vega were both on their way to Cozumel

Tulum in the early twentieth-century was populated by just a handful of Maya families, who all relied on subsistence agriculture, hunting, and chicle collecting to get by. By the mid-twentieth-century Tulum's residents also worked on the nearby coconut plantations and cattle ranches. By the 1960s and 1970s, the Maya *Cruzoob* descendants in Tulum began to be outnumbered by Yucatec and Mexican immigrants.

Soon thereafter, the tourism boom changed the Maya way of life in the Tulum area forever.

The *Culto de la Santa Cruz* (Cult of the Holy Cross) still maintains a *santuario,* or shrine, in downtown Tulum. Other towns, such as Chunpón, Xcacál Guardia, Chancáh Veracruz, San Antonio Muyil, and Felipe Carrillo Puerto also have active *santuarios* or *centros ceremoniales* of the cult. Adherents of the cult believe the crosses erected within the shrines are saints and are more powerful than the saints who have a human form. The cult members communicate with the crosses via handwritten notes, which a Maya priest interprets. Entry to the shrines is restricted, and the wearing of hats or shoes, or taking photographs is forbidden. To make sure these rules are obeyed, members of the *Guardia Del Santo*, a group organized in the same hierarchy as the *Cruzoob* rebels were during the War of the Castes, take turns guarding the sanctuary.

Archaeological expeditions to Tulum

The first non-Maya to visit and report on the ruins of Tulum was the Spanish militia captain Juan José Galvéz, in 1798. This report was paraphrased by the Yucatecan Mayanist Juan Pio Perez in 1840, but Pio did not visit the site himself and the original report by Galvéz was lost. In 1841, explorers John Lloyd Stephens and Frederick Catherwood cleared much of the forest away around the ruins so that Catherwood could draw them with the aid of a camera lucida, which they later published. In 1895, William Henry Holmes of the Field Columbian Museum in Chicago sketched drawings of Tulum from aboard Allison V. Armour's boat *Ituna* while he stayed safely offshore, fearful of actually landing there because of the Maya rebel activity. From their safe position on the boat, the expedition members saw rebels waving signal flags and beat a hasty retreat before even setting foot on dry land, just as Grijalva did in 1518. Later, in 1911, George Howe and William Parmelee of Harvard spent two days exploring the site, sleeping aboard their vessel offshore in case of attack.

Above: Sketch made by William Henry Holmes in 1895, showing the heavy vegetation covering Tulum at the time.

Sylvanus Morley and Jesse Nusbaum, of the School of American Research in Santa Fe, New Mexico, were the next to visit Tulum in 1913. They only stayed ashore for two hours, too worried that the Maya rebels would show up to stay longer. As they tried to leave, their boat turned turtle in the surf, and they lost most of the exposed glass negatives they had taken of the site.

The pair had been out of touch with their sponsors back in Santa Fe, New Mexico for so long by then, that rumors began circulating in the US newspapers that they had been eaten by cannibals. Morley returned to Tulum in 1916 as an investigator for the Carnegie Institute and, together with British amateur archaeologist Dr. Thomas Gann, he managed to get four days of work done there (their crew refused to come ashore) before they felt they were pushing their luck and departed. In 1918, Morley tried once more to make some headway at Tulum and then Prince William of Sweden made a one-day visit in 1920, where he met and had a conversation with some of the former *Cruzoob* whom he describe thusly: *"Their costume consisted of thin linen trousers, rolled up to the knee, and a ragged shirt. Their bodies were generally well-developed, but the faces bore a pained, degenerate expression, speaking eloquently of inbreeding and ill-health. Their complexion was a dusky brown, with a thin, stiff growth of beard on the chin. The chief and those nearest him wore gold ornaments in their ears, but only on the left side."*

Above: Archaeologist Sylvanus Griswold Morley, of the School for Advanced Research, Santa Fe, New Mexico, dressed for a costume party as a Maya priest in 1926!

Above: Jesse Nusbaum, the photographer who accompanied Sylvanus Morley to Tulum. Although he was not eaten by cannibals, he lost most of the glass negatives he shot in Tulum in 1913 when his boat turned over in the surf.

Above: Prince William of Sweden (tall man in the center wearing a pith helmet) surrounded by Cruzoob Maya at Tulum.

Sylvanus Morley visited Tulum again in 1922, when he reported finding the building of El Castillo swept clean and an 18-inch-tall wooden cross painted blue and dressed in cloth sitting on the bench against the wall with burnt candles all around it. More expeditions followed; Samuel Lothrop, Thomas Gann, Sylvanus Morley, and Oliver Ricketson paid a visit in 1923. When they walked up to the Castillo, they saw that it had been swept clean inside, and on a bench against the wall they found a small wooden cross, 16 to 18 inches high, painted blue and dressed with an embroidered *huipil*. In front of the cross the floor was covered with white, yellow and pink candle wax. The next day, twenty *Cruzoob* soldiers showed up and wanted to know what the strangers were up to. Satisfied with the explanation Morley gave them, they came back the next day and prayed at the Castillo.

Samuel Lothrop and Gregory Mason reached Tulum on a 1926 trip sponsored by the New York Times. They mention they only found burnt *copal*, or incense in the Castillo, but no cross. Thomas Gann returned in 1927 where he found several Maya praying in the Castillo, and took their photo.

Above: Maya praying inside El Castillo in 1927.

One of the most famous visitors to Tulum in those early days was Charles Lindbergh. After taking off from Cozumel in 1929 in his Pan American Airways Sikorsky S-38 amphibious plane, accompanied by his wife, Carnegie Institute's Dr. Ricketson, Dr. Alfred E. Kidder, W. I. Van Deusen, Charles Lorber, and William Ehmer, Lindbergh made a water landing in front of Tulum and visited the site for a few hours before taking off again. They later took aerial photographs of the jungle canopy in an effort to identify more ruin sites.

In 1937, the *Expedición Científica Mexicana* visited Tulum and Tancah. Beginning in 1938, Miguel Angel Fernández of the *Instituto Nacional de Antropologia e Historia (INAH)* spent several years excavating parts of the city and stabilizing the city wall and the buildings found within it. He also emptied the substructure of the Castillo, consolidated its walls and replaced the roof completely. *INAH* archaeologist Ignacio Marquina worked on the site in 1951. William Sanders worked all along the coast of Quintana Roo in 1955 and 1960, and was one of the first to reconstruct the time-line of the occupation of Tulum through ceramic evidence. In 1971, Arthur Miller began his studies of the murals in Tulum. Later, in 1974 and 1975, much more stabilization work was done under the auspices of *INAH*.

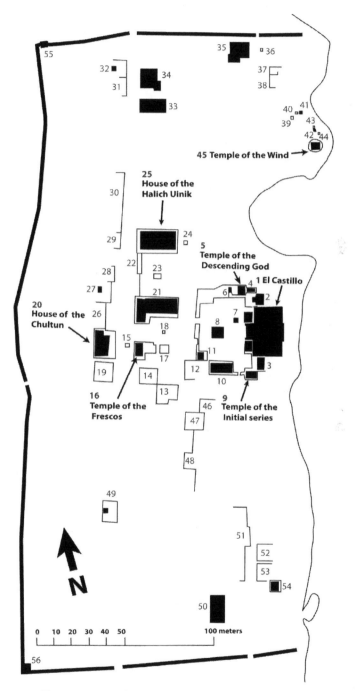

Above: A map of the ceremonial precinct of Tulum.

The Structures of Tulum

The first thing you will notice about Tulum is that it is surrounded by a thick stone wall. However, no matter what you hear, Tulum is not the only walled Maya city: Mayapán is the largest Maya walled city with over 5 miles of perimeter wall encompassing over 2.5 square miles within its protective enclosure. Ichpaatun has a wall system with a total length of about 5,000 feet enclosing roughly 67 acres. Becan had both a city wall and a moat. Xel-Ha, Cuca, Chacchob, Muna, and Dzonot Aké are among others that also have protective walls around them.

During the period we now call the Postclassic (from 1250 A.D. to the arrival of the Spanish in the 16th century) the independent Maya states in Yucatán had entered a period of constant warfare. The cities mentioned above all sought protection from attack buy surrounding themselves with high palisades. Tulum's wall is an impressive 20 feet thick in some places and ranges from 10 to 16 feet high and is over 2,000 feet long. There are 5 entrances that pierce the wall, 2 on the south, 2 on the north, and 1 on the west. *Sacbes*, or Maya ceremonial roads, radiated out into the countryside from all five of these entrances. There are also two watchtowers built into the wall, one in the northwest corner and one in the southwest corner. The wall was extensively restored and strengthened by *INAH* in 1974 and 1975.

The section of Tulum open to tourists today includes the ceremonial center and elite residential units that lie within the confines of the protective wall. Only the elite lived inside the wall; the rest of the Maya of pre-Conquest Tulum lived outside of these walls in a sprawling, but thinly populated, residential area stretching for over three miles up and down the coast.

All of the buildings standing inside the walls of Tulum date from the Postclassic Period, from 1250 A. D. to the arrival of the Spanish. The style of construction is termed "East Coast" and shows several traits common to other postclassic Quintana Roo Maya sites, such as negative batter (walls that slope slightly outward) and relatively crude stonework which was covered over by thick coats of plaster. The elite residential units in

Tulum follow the Mayapán style; inner rooms that include an altar and outer meeting areas with benches. The exterior adornments of the buildings are heavily influenced by the Toltec and Mixtec of Central Mexico, influences which also show Tulum was a city built by the Itzá Maya. The *Halach Uiniks* (Maya governors) who ruled Tulum were of the same royal lineage as the rulers of Cozumel (another Itzá Maya settlement) and there must have been close relationship between the two groups.

1 El Castillo

The name El Castillo (The Castle) was given to the building by Spaniards; the Maya did not call it that. It is the dominant building in Tulum and is a temple dedicated to Kukulcan, the feathered serpent man/god who the Maya believed founded the second phase of Chichen Itzá and later Mayapán. The great pyramid at Chichen Itzá was also a temple dedicated to Kukulcan and the two buildings show similar feathered-snake motifs. Maya tradition holds that he was a stranger who had come out of the west and they associated him with the planet Venus, which the Maya called Xux ek, the "wasp star."

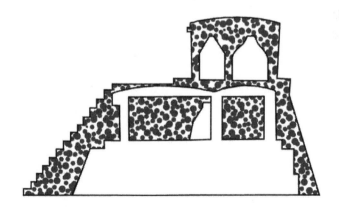

The original building was filled with rubble (except for a passageway running north to south along the inner wall) and a new temple built atop of the old one.

The edifice was built in three different stages, in which newer sections were built over older sections. The only parts of the earliest stage that can be seen now are the north and south wings; the old central part of the structure was filled in with rubble and used as a base on which to construct the staircase and temple above you see today. The third stage of construction consisted of the addition of the small north and south shrines that were added to the front of the building.

The choice of the location of El Castillo would seem at first glance to be obvious; the commanding position atop the cliff face. However, beneath the building lies the real reason for its exact placement; it was built over a sacred, natural cave. When it was partially excavated in the 1970s by Lourdes Martínez Guzmán and William Folan, burials and grave-goods were discovered inside. American Bob Marx, a legendary treasure hunter, scuba diver and raconteur tells a yarn that includes the statement that he buried 350 pounds of gold in the cave in the 1950s.

Above: The temple atop El Castillo, in a photo by Jesse Nusbaum in 1913.

Three niches adorn the façade of the room atop El Castillo. The central niche holds a plaster representation of the Descending God (sometimes incorrectly called the *Diving* God), a late postclassic aspect of the god Kukulcan embodied as the planet Venus. He is shown here in the "descending" aspect that the Maya employed to illustrate his "coming down from heaven," the time of the year that Venus first appears as the morning star. This Tulum version of Descending God is identical to other late postclassic depictions of the god found in Mayapán, Coba, and Sayil. 1930s Archaeologist Ralph Roys had his own opinion, which associates this plaster image with Muzen Cab, the Bee God, based mainly on the similarity between the depictions of Xux ek (Wasp Star) and Muzen Cab (Bee God).

Above: The postclassic Descending God appearing as Xux Ek, the Wasp Star.

Above: The Maya Bee Deity, Muzen Cab.

Many guides and books now repeat Roy's 1930s theory as gospel. However, Bishop Landa recorded in his 1566 book, *Relaciónes de las cosas de Yucatán,* that the Maya believed that after Kukulkán established Mayapán, he returned to his own land and then "went up to heaven as a god and became the planet Venus." Previously, the Classic Period Maya god we now call "God I" (called Tzontemoc by the Aztecs) was the one associated with Venus, but he was replaced by the postclassic Maya with this new feathered-serpent god, Kukulkán, especially in the Itzá cities of Chichen Itzá, Tulum, Coba, and Mayapán.

In Mayapán, there is a wall connected to Kukulkán's temple that bears a series of murals depicting two men carrying banners, flanking an image of the "Descending God." More images of this "Descending God" as Xux Ek appear in the Dresden Codex, where the head of the god is drawn as "*ek,*" the glyph for "star." Further, when one considers that the Maya festival of *Chic Kaban,* honoring Kukulkán, was celebrated on the first appearance of Venus and the fact that El Castillo in Tulum was built to contain alignment elements that coincide with this celestial event, identifying the Descending God with Kukulkán is much more reasonable than connecting him with the Maya Bee God, simply because the two depictions have wings.

There have been many other, even more far-out interpretations of the identity of the Descending God at Tulum. Some "esoteric, mystic, knowledge-seekers" have postulated the image was placed there by descendants of the Merovingians, the Frank dynasty that some claim carried the bloodline the descendants of Jesus. Other goof-balls claim that the headdress the god wears is actually a space helmet, proving that Tulum was founded by little alux-like aliens from outer space who were later worshiped by the Maya. Tulum tour guides are often quoted as saying the figure is the "diving god" and that he is the god of Scuba diving. Still others claim that only the Illuminati know the true identity of the Descending God, and they're not telling.

Above: El Castillo as it appeared in Catherwood's book.

Just because Ralph Roys' bee-god theory is all wet, is not to say apiculture was not very important to the Maya. At the time of the European discovery of America, the common honeybee (a native of Europe) was unknown in Yucatán and the only bees found here were the Yucatán stingless bees (such as *Meliponini beecheii* and *M. Yucatánica*). Maya farmers kept these bee colonies in short hollow logs stoppered with stone discs that they housed in small, circular, stone enclosures. The honey was used as the base ingredient of a ceremonial alcoholic beverage, called *balché*, a potent drink flavored with the bark of the *balché* tree *(Lonchocarpus violaceus)*, wild tobacco *(Nicotiana sylvestris)*, and sometimes the hallucinogenic secretions of the cane toad *(Bufo marinas)*. The honey used to brew the *balché* was slightly hallucinogenic itself; the Yucatán stingless bees which harvest nectar from plants that produce psychoactive compounds, such as the *tajonal (Viguiera dentata)*, *tzitzilché (Gymnopodium floribundum)*, and *xtabentún (Turbina corymbosa)*, pass these compounds on to the honey in an unaltered state.

Ralph Roys and the esoteric mystics were not the only ones to come up with an unusual theory of the true identity of the Descending God over the doorway of this temple. Some Mormons believe this plaster image is actually a representation of Jesus Christ after he was supposed to have visited the New World after his resurrection. These particular Mormons also believe that the northern niche holds an image of God the Father and, since there is nothing left in the southern niche, they say it represents the invisible Holy Ghost.

LDS church members offer their own tours of Tulum. The guides to these tours closely toe the line as far relating the history of Tulum so that it dovetails with Mormon mythology. One of the more grievous examples of the twisting of the true history of the site to fit LDS theology is the Mormon claim that Tulum was an important, thriving walled city 367 days after the crucifixion of Christ, which has been customarily dated to around 2,000 years ago. Archaeological evidence proves that Tulum was not in existence as a city and the wall was not built until around 1200 AD. Another falsehood that is touted by the LDS guides is that their prophet Joseph Smith wrote that the name of the walled city of the Nephites was Zama. In reality, that claim only exists on websites and popular LDS books and never appeared in print until the late twentieth-century. Smith himself never penned the name Zama at any point in his life.

The LDS guides will also claim that the image of "the descending god" can only be found in Tulum. In truth, the image appears at many Yucatecan Maya postclassic sites, such as Coba, Sayil, and Mayapán, as well as the Dresden Codex.

Many other such garbled interpretations of the history of Yucatán are made by the LDS guides to make it conform to the Book of Mormon, but the truth is, Tulum was simply a postclassic Maya city and had nothing to do with the mythological Nephites or Lamanites.

In 1985, I took part in the "Tulum Lighthouse Project," a project of the *Instituto Nacional de Antropología e Historia (INAH)* which was underwritten by the National Geographic Society and the Kempner Fund. The project was the idea of Michael Creamer, an American who came up with the theory that the twin window/vent holes on the ocean-facing side of the building in Tulum known as "El Castillo" could act as a sort of range light system for Maya canoes attempting to cross over the reef at night to land on the beach next to the building.

Above: The seaward side of El Castillo, showing the two small openings.

To help test the theory, I borrowed a dugout canoe that had washed up on the beach at Cozumel and that Arturo Becerra was using as decoration in front of his restaurant on Avenida Melgar. A good friend of mine, Bill Horn, took the canoe to Tulum, along with all the supplies we would need for the time we would be staying at *INAH's* base camp the institute maintained just north of the beach by El Castillo. Other members of the team included *INAH* archaeologists Pilar Luna and Santiago Analco, Texas A&M School of Oceanography graduate student Vel Lena Steed, Michael Creamer, Aqua Safari dive shop owner Bill Horn, and divers Pamela Holden and my wife, Marie-France Lemire.

Creamer believed that by building a fire within the small uppermost room atop El Castillo, the Maya had utilized the beams of lights from the two 18-inch-wide openings on the side of the building facing the sea as range lights for an aid to navigation. Because of the thickness of the wall in which the openings were set, the beams of light they projected could only be seen when one looked directly into them. If one was not lined up <u>exactly</u> perpendicular to the back wall of the building and these openings, the lights were not visible. The reef in front of Tulum, Michael reasoned, must have been dangerous for Maya canoes to negotiate at night, but if these range lights could help them align their canoe with an opening in the reef directly in front of El Castillo, they could paddle through the pass and land safely. That was the theory.

The first thing Pam and I did after camp was set up was to take our zodiac out to the area where Creamer believed the pass through the reef lay and mark it with buoys.   We found a spot in the reef in front of El Castillo that was deeper than the rest of the reef; however, although it offered over 10 feet of clearance between the surface of the sea and the sea-floor, it was only slightly deeper than the reef on either side of the passage. Unless Maya canoes had a draft of over 7 feet, they would not necessarily be obliged to use this pass; they could simply glide over other parts of the reef just as easily.

In the early 1990s in Rio Belen, (a small village in Veraguas, Panama), I had a group of fellows cut down a huge *bateo* tree and carve a 45-foot-long dug-out canoe from its trunk for me. We attached a 45-horsepower outboard motor to this canoe (which I christened the *Don Tiki*) and I travelled all along the coast of Panama in it, from Costa Rica to Colombia. Even when the canoe was heavily laden with 55-gallon drums of gasoline and crates of supplies, it drew less than two feet of water. I frequently surfed this 45-foot-long craft through the breakers and over shallow sand bars as we entered the mouths of rivers and I never had a problem because of the draft of the vessel. Even if you could <u>double</u> the length of the canoe and make it 100 feet long, the draft would not increase proportionately; it would never be more than around two or three feet.

The next thing we did at Tulum for the experiment was to wait until after sunset and place a gas lantern inside the small room atop El Castillo. We were not allowed to make a fire within the room, as *INAH* felt that the smoke and soot produced by the fire would smudge the walls and ceiling. This got me to thinking; if the Maya had built nightly fires within this room so that the light could be seen out to sea, after a short period, the inside of the room would look as blackened and soot-caked as the inside of a fireplace. Why were there <u>absolutely no visible signs</u> of soot or carbon on the walls or in the cracks of the plaster? Granted, we did not take core samples, which would offer the ultimate test of the presence of soot (or lack thereof), but we didn't see any. The inside of the room was well protected from the elements. The Maya could not have simply scrubbed the residue off of the porous plaster and stone; some traces of it must necessarily remain if fires or torches were ever used inside the room. But we saw none. Besides that, if a fire had been built in the room, the heat rising from it would have eventually damaged the ceiling, which was made of limestone and not very heat-resistant.

After we placed the lantern in El Castillo, I took the 12-foot-long dugout canoe that we brought from Cozumel and paddled it out past the reef. As I paddled back and forth in the dark in a line parallel with the back wall of El Castillo, I would see first the light from one window appear, then as I paddled a little farther, the light from the second window would also appear. If I continued to paddle in the same direction, the first light would disappear, then after a few more yards, the second one would go dark. The next thing to do was to see if the patch of ocean where I could see both lights at the same time was directly over the pass we previously marked in the reef. We attached strobe lights to the buoys marking the pass and I tried again. The lights coming from El Castillo were aligned with the space between the buoys.

After we finished the experiment, I could not help but face the insurmountable problem of the lack of any trace of soot in the room, the lack of any signs of heat cracks or heat damage to the walls or ceiling, and the fact that the Maya canoes were not necessarily restricted to using only the pass to approach the beach to land because of their draft. I was not the only one with doubts. In the report Creamer wrote and later published in the Institute of Nautical Archaeology (INA) newsletter, he stated: "It is unlikely that we can prove how Maya mariners actually used Tulum's Castillo Tower..." Creamer went on to say in the report that the experiment only "... demonstrated that vessels with a draft of more than 7 feet" would be obliged to use the pass through the reef.

Be all that as it may be, the story of our experiment took on a life of its own. Creamer later re-enacted the experiment (I did not take part) in 1998 for Arthur C. Clarke's *Mysterious Universe –The Mysterious Maya* for Discovery Channel. At the end of the program, he states, *"As far as I'm concerned, we have proved it."* Later, in 2009, the program was shown on the Spanish version of the History Channel. A posting was even made on Wikipedia, stating the experiment we conducted *"...conclusively proved that Tulum's El Castillo served as an aid to navigating the narrow gap in the offshore coral reef."* Today, this theory has evolved into a "fact" that is deeply entrenched in the collective belief of the people who saw these TV programs and read the Wikipedia entry. Undoubtedly, at some point during your visit to Tulum, you will hear someone repeat this revisionist version of the results of the experiment.

Above: The Temple of the Descending God by Catherwood from Views of Ancient Monuments Central America, Chiapas and Yucatán.

5 The Temple of the Descending God

Once again, the Tulum Maya chose to fill-in a temple and construct a new one on top of it. The newer, uppermost part of the temple once had a painted mural running around the top of its façade, and was also adorned within with murals depicting the sky and gods associated with the heavens. The interior also was covered in murals depicting gods of the heavens in the night sky. The eastern window is situated so that a beam of light passes through it to illuminate a section of the mural on the morning of the winter solstice. The structure is named after the sculpture of the Descending God Kukulkán in his aspect of the wasp star it bears on its facade.

The entire façade were once painted with images. A series of interlaced serpents formed a series of squares containing images of gods; remnants remain of the gods of the sun, rain and corn. The interior eastern wall held a mural framed by a band representing the night sky with Venus and various stars with interlaced serpents.

9 The Temple of the Initial Series

John L. Stevens found a broken stela (carved, stone marker) in 1841 bearing the Mayan Long Count date of 564 A. D. lying in front of the platform altar next to this building. It had undoubtedly been transported to Tulum from some other location (probably Coba, a much older site) as Tulum had not been occupied that far back in the past. In 1911, when George Howe and William Parmelee of Harvard came to Tulum, they attempted to drag the stone to the beach and load it aboard their boat, but gave up because it was too heavy and buried it in the sand. When Sylvanus Morley and Jesse Nussbaum, of the School of American Research in Santa Fe, New Mexico came to Tulum in 1916, they dug the stela out of the sand, photographed it, and re-buried it. Later the same year, Morley returned to Tulum, this time working for the Carnegie Institute but also on the payroll of the US Naval Intelligence as a spy. He was tasked with keeping a look out for German activity along the coast of Yucatán, under the cover of his archaeological work. It is not unlikely that he was the inspiration for the film character "Indiana Jones."

Morley was accompanied by Thomas Gann, a British amateur archaeologist, and Gann later returned in 1926 and dug up the stela for the last time, carrying it back to the British Museum in London, where it still resides. Another old stela was similarly moved from the neighboring Late Classic Period site of Tancah to Tulum by the Maya in the Postclassic Period.

Above: Stela 1 that was found in Tulum, now in the British Museum

The term "initial series" comes from the notation system the Maya used in which they placed an "introductory" or "initial" glyph immediately preceding the numbers that indicate a long-count date so that the string of numbers can be identified as a calendar date and not just a string of numbers. The term "long count" describes the perpetual calendar of the Maya and other Mesoamerican cultures.

One of the earliest Mesoamerican societies was the Olmec, a group that had its origins on the gulf coast of Mexico over 4,500 years ago and later spread southwards across the Isthmus of Tehuantepec. The early Olmec were the first Mesoamerican society to develop writing and it was this ability that allowed them to record the passage of time in a manner which would evolve first into a 260 day calendar, then a 365-day calendar, and later a system that today we call "The Mesoamerican Long Count." Later, as other Mesoamerican cultures, including the Aztec, Toltec, Mixtec, and the Maya began to develop, they each adopted these earlier Olmec calendars as their own.

The first calendar system developed by the Olmec was the 260 day "ritual" calendar. The earliest evidence of this 260-day calendar is in Monte Alban, on Stelae 12 and 13, both made over 2,500 years ago.

One theory of its origin was that the Olmec based it on the length of the average human pregnancy, counting from the date of the first missed menstruation. The fact that this ritual calendar was integrally linked with the ritual naming Mesoamerican children lends some credence to this theory. The ancient Maya goddess Ix Chel also was closely associated with both childbirth and the calendar and this calendar is still used today by mid-wives in parts of Guatemala to predict the date pregnant women will give birth. Other theories on the origin of the 260-day calendar abound, but each has their own Achilles heel.

The ancient Yucatec Maya adopted this 260-day Olmec calendar and used it to schedule many of their ceremonies as well as an aid to assigning names to their children. Today, we call this calendar the *tzolk'in*, a Maya compound word meaning "count of days." No one knows for sure what the pre-Hispanic Maya called it. The Aztecs also adopted this Olmec calendar, which they renamed the *tonalpohualli*.

The calendar was made up of 20 named days and 13 day numbers, which were combined in a way to form the 260 distinctly named days. After the Olmec created the 260 day calendar, they went on to develop a 365-day "Solar-year" calendar, based on the earth's rotation around the Sun. This calendar was divided into 18 months, each made up of 20 days, plus a 19th month made up of only 5 days, which the Maya later named the *wayeb'*. This 365-day calendar is now called the *haab'* calendar in Mayan and the *xiuhpohualli* in Nahuatl, the language of the Aztec.

Combining the dates generated by the 260-day ritual calendar with those of the 365-day Solar-year calendar, the Maya could create 18,980 unique dates, enough for 52-years. After that, the dates began repeating themselves. This combination of the *tzolk'in* and *haab'* calendars is called a "Calendar Round" or the *tunben k'ak*, meaning "binding the years" in Mayan.

The Long Count, unlike the Calendar Round, is a <u>linear</u> way to keep track of time and to assign each day a unique identity. It is simply a tally of the number of days from a fixed starting point. The days (*k'in* in Mayan) within the Long Count are divided into groups of 20 days (which the Maya called a *uinal*), 18 *unials* (making a *tun*, or 360 days), and 20 *tuns* (making a *k'atun*), and 20 *k'tuns* (making a *b'ak'tun* of 144,000 days, or about 394 years). Once the end of a *b'ak'tun* is reached, the Long count begins adding the number of days, *uinals, tuns, k'atuns*, after the new *b'ak'tun* number, just like we do at the turn of a millennium.

2012 marked the end of the 13th *b'ak'tun*. Remember all the fuss about 2012 and the end of the world BS? The system was designed to continue with a 14th *b'ak'tun,* 15th *b'ak'tun,* 16th *b'ak'tun*, and so on, up to 20 *b'ak'tuns*. Cycles longer than 20 *b'ak'tuns* can be counted in the Maya Long Count, with *pik'túns* (or 20 *bak'túns*, about 7,885 years), a *kalab'túns* (or 20 *piktuns*, about 157,703 years), *kinch'il'túns* (or 20 *kalab'túns*, about 3.2 million years), *alautúns* (or 20 *kinch'il'túns*, about

64 million years), and the *hablatún* (or 20 *alautúns*, about 1.26 billion years). The Maya had never anticipated an end to their calendar; it was designed to be perpetual.

Where did the start date for the Long Count come from? The *Popol Vuh*, a compilation of Maya creation myths of the Quiché Maya of Guatemala, describes how three different worlds were created by the gods and then destroyed by them because of imperfections. The book states that the gods then created a fourth world, the one in which they placed the Maya. The Maya marked the point in time in which they believed the fourth world began by projecting back and using it as the starting point of the current Long Count period we find ourselves in today. This current Long Count cycle was begun 13 *b'ak'tuns* ago, on *0.0.0.0.0 4 Ajaw 8 Kumk'u* (August 11, 3114 BC according to the modified G.M.T. correlation; more about that later). This date is over 2,500 years BEFORE any evidence of a Maya culture.

How many *b'ak'tuns* did the Maya believe each of the previous 3 worlds lasted? We have no record of their views regarding the amount of time each of the previous incarnations of the world endured, only that the Maya believed they had existed prior to this current world's incarnation. So, why would anyone think that the Maya believed that this fourth incarnation of the world would come to an end upon the completion of the Long Count's 13th *b'ak'tun* (or the date of 13.0.0.0.0) of this current Long Count? This belief may come from a misunderstanding of the Maya "New Fire Ceremony," a ceremony that they, as well as every other Mesoamerican society, held at the end of every 52-year calendar round.

The Maya *did* believe there would be an end to this present world. They just weren't sure exactly when it would come. Prophecies mentioned in the *Chilam Balam of Tizimín* and other sources indicate they believed that when the end of the world came, it would coincide with the ending of a 52-year Calendar Round. Consequently, the last day of every Calendar Round, the Maya would clean out their houses, break up old utensils, and put out all hearth fires while they waited for the first day of the next 52-year round to begin. At the dawn of the first day of the new round, a

"New Fire Ceremony" would be held to celebrate the fact that the world had not ended after all. New fires were lit in the temples and each household would carry a burning ember home from these sacred fires to start new hearth-fires, symbolizing a new beginning.

The idea that the Maya were more concerned about the end of *b'ak'tun* 13 than the ending of any other *b'ak'tun* is belied by the fact that they never mentioned this date in any of their writings (that have been found) except for one, possibly two, very obscure mentions that say nothing about any calamity.

Structure 13

This low platform holds two graves with vaulted ceilings.

Structure 15

This small altar is where the pieces of Stela 2 were found. The inscription on the stela *(2 Ahau)* is not a complete date, but the only year during the Late Postclassic Period that has that date combination is 1263 A. D., according to the Maya calendar round. The style of the engraving matches well with this date.

16 Temple of the Frescos

Once more, the Maya used an old temple building for a base on which to build another. The old, original temple which now forms the inner chamber of the first floor was richly painted with murals. The front façade has three niches that hold a stucco image of the descending god in the center niche, flanked by seated figures with elaborate headdresses on either side. Between the niches are decorations of a man enveloped in an interlacing snake or cord motif.

The upper floor exhibits a pronounced negative batter; that is, the walls are angled outward at the top. This is a very common architectural feature in East Coast postclassic buildings. The façade of the upper temple room sports a niche that once held a stucco image of the descending god, and a row of moldings between which were painting of other gods and intertwined serpents. The paintings in this temple, dating to about 1450, so resemble the style of the images in the Paris, Madrid, and Dresden Codices (the only three Mayan books that managed to escape being burned by zealous Spanish priests) that some archaeologists believe the codices was created in, or nearby, Tulum. However, there is more evidence that points to one or more of the Codices being originally made in Cozumel.

Four months after Hernán Cortés arrived in Veracruz, on the road to conquer the Aztec capital of Tenochtitlan, he sent a shipload of pillaged loot back to Spain, part of which was the "Royal Fifth," or the 20% share of the plunder taken during the conquest that was owed as tax to the Spanish Crown. Along with the plunder, Cortés sent a letter from Veracruz dated July 10, 1519; a letter now known as his *"Primera carta de relación."* In the missive, Cortés lists in detail all of the items he was sending back to the royal court, including *"two books of the kind the Indians here have."*

Although this is the first ever mention of pre-Colombian codices, there were more to come. *Hispania Victrix: segunda parte de la historia general de las Indias* is the book Francisco López de Gomara, Hernando Cortés' private secretary, published in 1552 detailing Cortés' conquest of México. In his account, Gomara describes in great detail the collection of gold, silver, and art that comprised the Royal Fifth shipment of 1519, and also mentions that a group of six captive Indians from the Totonac capital Cempoala were sent along as well. But, most interestingly, Gomara says that the shipment also included *"some books containing figures as letters, used by the Mexicans, cryptographs on canvass, with writings all over. Some were made of cotton and paste, and others of agave leaves that served as paper."*

Gomara's description of the materials used in the construction of some of the books was somewhat confused; the folded panels were actually made of the processed bark of the *ficus* tree (a paper the Maya called *kopó*) rather than cotton fiber, and the surface treatment was gesso, not starch paste. The Maya called these screen-folded books *hu'un*. Regardless of the slight errors in his description of the books, it is very clear that what Gomara was describing were accordion-folded, Maya codices.

After being inventoried at *Casa de Contratación* in Sevilla, the loot (including the codices and the captured nobles) was moved to the royal court in Valladolid. There, in March of 1520, Pietro Martire de'Anghiera (who is known as Peter Martyr in English) examined the codices, along with Giovanni Ruffo a Forli, who was the archbishop of Cosenza and the Pope's representative in Valladolid. Although Martyr did not write about the codices until a few years later, Archbishop Ruffo did, in a letter he immediately fired off to Francesco Chieragati of Rome, dated March 7, 1520. In the letter, the Archbishop says *"I had forgotten to say that there were some paintings less than a palm's span in height that were folded into the form of a book, which when unfolded, stretched out. In these little books, figures and signs in the form of Arabic and Egyptian letters have been interpreted to be their letters, and the Indians had no idea what they meant."*

The Indians who the Archbishop said had no idea what the books contained, were the six Indian nobles who had been captured by the Totonacs of Cempoala and turned over to Cortés, who had then sent them to Valladolid as part of the Royal Fifth. It was no surprise that they couldn't read the glyphs in the texts; these Indian nobles were from the central part of México and were only familiar with deerskin codices illustrating Aztec, Mexica, Totonac, Chinantec, or Zapotec mythology written and illustrated by scribes of that area; the screen-folded *kopó* codices that formed part of the Royal Fifth were written in Maya glyphs and dealt with Maya mythologies and Maya astronomical calculations, something these fellows knew nothing about.

The notion that the codices in the Royal Fifth were made by the Maya is supported by the later writings of Peter Martyr. As the historian for King Ferdinand and Queen Isabella, Martyr proved his worth when he interviewed Cristóbal Colón and several of his crew and recorded what the explorers experienced during the first voyages to the New World in his book *De Orbe Novo*, which details the earliest years of the Spanish exploration of America. Martyr later added five additional chapters, or *Decades*, to that book, chapters dealing with the history of the Spanish conquest of the New World. In Decade Four, Martyr describes what Hernán Cortés and his expedition found when they set foot on Mexican soil for the first time as they landed on Cozumel in February of 1519: *"Our people found themselves among various unoccupied houses, and availed themselves of the food of the land, and found adornments of various colors in the houses, tapestries, clothing, and coverlets of rustic cotton that they call Amaccas. They also have, O Holy Father, innumerable books. Of these and the other things which they brought to our new Caesar [King Charles] we shall tell of further on."*

As promised, later in the book Martyr describes the codices: *"What they write upon are some sheets of a certain thin inner tree bark which grows underneath the outer bark... where there is a hard cloth that separates the layers... when they are soft, they give them the form that they desire and spread them out at their discretion, and then to harden them they coat them, one supposes with plaster or some similar material."*

Martyr goes on to add: *"Not only do they bind their books, but they also stretch out this material many cubits, and reduce it to square sections, not loose, but so united... [so that] whenever one looks at an open book, the two written faces are displayed; two pages appear, and under these are hidden another two as it is not stretched out at length, but underneath one folio are many other joined folios."*

Peter Martyr had never been to the New World and the Indian captives he interviewed at Valladolid couldn't tell him anything about the books. So, how could he go into such detail about their manufacture and the materials of which they were made? The answer is that when Cortés sent the Royal Fifth back to Spain in 1519, it was accompanied by one of the conquistador's men, Francisco de Montejo, who had been to Yucatán earlier with Francisco Hernández de Córdoba in 1517 and to Cozumel with Juan de Grijalva in 1518. Montejo was surely familiar with the Maya use and manufacture of *ficus*-bark codices, and it is known for certain that Martyr interviewed him at length during the four years Montejo remained in Valladolid. Now, the next question is, if the codices that were shipped to Spain as part of the Royal Fifth were Maya in origin, where in the Maya realm did Cortés get them? The most plausible answer is Cozumel.

Cortés' expedition came to the island directly from Cuba in February of 1519 and stayed on Cozumel for several days, interacting peacefully with the Maya there and exchanging many gifts with them. When he left the island on his way to Veracruz, his second landing in México was at Isla Mujeres, which expedition member Bernal Díaz de Castillo said they found abandoned. López de Gomara wrote that in Isla Mujeres *"Cortés landed to ascertain the lay of the land and the disposition of the people, but he didn't like it much."* They then said a Mass on Isla Mujeres before sailing away.

The third stop was in the anchorage in front of Campeche, but Gomara and Díaz both say that they did not go ashore there and had no interaction with the Maya. Later, they moved on to *"a large bay that is now known as Puerto Escondido"* where they hunted rabbits but found no Indians with whom they could trade. The expedition's next stop was Potonchán at the mouth of Rio Tabasco, (not Champotón, Campeche, as often reported), where they fought with the Indians they encountered there. Gomara says that after the battle the Indians gifted the Spaniards with food, 400 pesos worth of small jewelry, some small pieces of low quality turquoise, and twenty slaves. But in any regard, Potonchán was a city of the Chontal Maya, not the Yucatec Maya. These two groups speak different languages and have different customs, and the images, glyphs, and rituals in the Codex are all typical of the Yucatec Maya. All the expedition's stops after Potonchán were in territories that belonged to non-Maya Indians, so it is doubtful that a Maya codex would have been acquired in any of those areas, either.

Many archaeologists and ethnologists have noted the similarity between the styles of the drawings and glyphs in the Dresden, Madrid and Paris

Codices and those appearing in the murals in the Late Postclassic Maya ruins at Playa del Carmen, Tulum, and Tancah, three Maya cities that had very close political and religious ties with pre-Columbian Cozumel. Many have gone as far as to hypothesize that one or more of these codices were created in one of these locations, based upon these similarities. Unfortunately, no Maya temple murals have survived on Cozumel, but there is no reason to believe they would not be similar, if not identical, to those of the cities on the adjacent mainland, and by corollary, to the Dresden Codex.

So, if the Dresden, Madrid or Paris Codices were included in the two books that made up part of the Royal Fifth of 1519, it seems clear that they had to have come from Cozumel.

The murals in the Temple of the Frescos depict the Maya god Itzamná and the moon goddess Ix Chel holding two small Chacs, or rain gods. In front of the temple is a small altar and stela with a date of 1263. Another god depicted here is the Aztec war god Tezcatlipoca.

Above: The Temple of the Frescos by Catherwood from Incidents of Travel in Yucatán.

Ix Chel was an important goddess to the Putún/Itzá, and there were also shrines dedicated to her in Cozumel. The Spanish wrote that the most common offering made at Ix Chel's shrines was dog. The Maya priests would rip out the pooch's beating heart, burn it in front of the temple dedicated to the goddess, then cook the rest of the canine in a stew of corn and chili peppers.

If you believe everything you read put out by the tourism boards, the island of Cozumel was home to a great temple dedicated to Ix Chel with a giant hollow statue of the goddess, in which Maya priests would hide inside and pretend to make prophecies by faking her voice. These tourist boards, and others, also claim that every Maya woman would make a pilgrimage to Cozumel at least once in her lifetime. Today, there is even an annual "recreation" of this pilgrimage with volunteers paddling dugout canoes from the mainland to Cozumel and back. However, this story is hogwash.

This myth originated in the twentieth century, mostly based on poor interpretations of early Spanish documents. The early documents and letters are clear; the Island of Cozumel was an important center for sacrifices to MANY Maya gods, not just Ix Chel. In fact, in all the pre-twentieth century documents, codices, or inscriptions in stone, there is only ONE document that includes mentions of both Cozumel and Ix Chel, and that was written by a Spaniard who says he is just retelling something he heard that happened many years ago. There are many more documents that talk about the other gods worshiped on Cozumel, but none of them mention Ix Chel at all.

The early documents that do mention Ix Chel never say that she was the goddess of fertility; that is another myth. She was the goddess of the act of childbirth, not of sex or fertility. The truth is, all these Ix Chel legends began after the first quarter of the twentieth century, and the websites and tourist boards have happily repeated them without ever checking their sources. For more information about this "Disneyfication" of Cozumel's past, read my book, The True History of Cozumel.

Above: The Temple of the Frescos in a 1913 photo by Jesse Nusbaum.

19 Funerary Platform

This platform contains a cross-shaped grave. Offerings of food was found next to the skeleton. The vessels contained trace of shark, iguana, crocodile, dove, turkey, heron, peccary, and conch.

20 House of the Chultun,

This structure is named after the *chultun*, or water storage pit, found at its southeast corner. The Maya made small channels in the plaster pavement that once covered most of the confines of the walled area, so rainwater would drain into these storage pits. This was an elite residential building (palace) with a two-column portico and a long inner gallery with a small covered shrine in the center. A room was added later to the northern end of the gallery. The entire palace was covered with a flat, wooden beam and mortar roof, which collapsed in the late 1920s. Over the doorways were niches with stucco images of the descending god. In the etching below, you can see John Stephens and Frederick Catherwood holding a tape measure across the front of the building, while their Maya crew cuts trees and clears the scrub surrounding the structure.

Above: Frederick Catherwood's 1841 drawing of the House of the Chultun.

21 The Great Palace

This was the largest elite residence in Tulum. The L-shaped structure was covered by a wooden beam and mortar roof. The window openings were barred with X-shaped stone bars, and stone rings were placed on either side of the interior doors so curtains could be hung to allow privacy.

25 Palace of the Halach Uinik

This elite residence also has a colonnaded portico and a roofed shrine in the interior. The doorway to the inner room has a niche with a stucco image of the descending god. This was the residence of the *Halach Uinik* ("True Man," in Mayan), the uppermost authority in Tulum. The last *Halach Uiniks* of the city were of the Pat lineage, a family that included the ruler of Cozumel as well. Subservient to the leader of Tulum and living inside the walls of the city, were his *Batab* (war captain) his *A'kin* (high priest), the *tupiles* (similar to sheriffs), the *nacom* (warriors), and the *akinoob* (priests). When the Spanish arrived in Yucatán, the total number of individuals making up this elite population numbered around 300. Living outside the walls were the *ppolm* (merchants), the *chembal uinikoob* (the common folk), and the *p'entacoob* (slaves).

Another colonnaded elite residence, the Great Palace (21), is located due north. A platform (22) connects the two residences. Under this platform lie two tombs.

Structures 26 through 30

These were all platforms that once held altars or small shrines, with steps leading up to them from street level.

Structure 34

This was either a two-room temple or small palace. It had a porch with two columns and the inner room held a roofed shrine. To the south of this structure lies Platform 33.

35 House of the Cenote

This small three-room building was erected over a cenote. All the water from the interior of the walled area of Tulum drains to this site, which is a naturally-formed sinkhole. The water at the bottom is brackish and was not used for drinking. The Maya believed these natural, karst openings in the bedrock were entrances to the underworld. Many have been excavated and found to contain offerings the Maya threw into them. Sometimes these offerings were ceramic vessels with a "kill hole" chipped into them so that they could only be used by the gods, sometimes the offerings were balls of copal incense or wooden implements, and sometime they were the remains of human sacrificial victims.

Structures 39 thorough 44

These were all small oratories, or chapels. These low, small buildings were very common along the coast, and are probably the origin of the legend of the Aluxes; small imaginary creatures similar to leprechauns. They were strictly symbolic and were not intended to be large enough for someone to crawl inside. Many had plaster statues of seated figures inside at one time. Stone phalli were found near these in Tulum, suggesting they were connected to some sort of fertility rite.

45 Temple of the Wind

The structure now known as the Temple of the Wind was built atop a circular platform, an architectural element imported into the peninsula by the Itzá and closely associated with temples erected in honor of K'uk'ulkan, in his "wind god" aspect. It is recorded in the codex Telleriano-Remensis that adulterers were killed at the wind god's altar.

Structure 54

This small temple is a one-room building atop square platform. It had a beam and mortar roof.

55 and 56, The Watchtowers

These two one-room watchtowers are almost identical, with three doorways and an altar set against the northern walls. Both buildings were decorated with murals on the exterior walls. Although they are commonly called "watchtowers," they are more appropriately considered small temples and did not serve a defensive "look out" function.

Above: Watchtower at Tulum by Catherwood

Your Diploma

So, now when you take your tour of Tulum you can look at the site with a different understanding, a new point of view. I am sure many tour guides will dispute some of the information I have chosen to include in this book, but that is often the way it is with information that flies in the face of traditional stories that have been told and re-told so often by websites and tour guides they seem to be carved in stone (pun intended!). My feeling is that the <u>true history</u> of a place is always more interesting than the made-up tales that seem to be the standard offering of tour guides in sites where tourists flock. Enjoy your tour, graduates!

Certification of Completion

With this certificate and a copy of the *True History of Tulum* in hand, you are hereby qualified as a

TULUM TOUR GUIDE

Suggested Reading

Aldana, Gerardo, "K'uk'ulkan at Mayapán: Venus and postclassic Maya statecraft," in *Journal for the History of Astronomy*, Vol. 34, Part 1, 2003

Allen, Joseph L. & Allen, Blake J., Exploring the Lands of the Book of Mormon, 2008

Catherwood, Frederick, Views of Ancient Monuments in Central America, Chiapas and Yucatan, 1844

Coe, David, The Maya, 1999

Farriss, Nancy M. & Miller, Arthur G., "Maritime culture contact of the Maya: underwater surveys and test excavations in Quintana Roo, Mexico" in *International Journal of Nautical Archaeology* Volume 6, Issue 2, 1977

Fernández, Miguel Ángel,
"Las Ruinas de Tulum I," *Anales de Museo Nacional de Historia y Etnografía*, 1945
"Las Ruinas de Tulum II," *Anales de Museo Nacional de Historia y Etnografía*, 1945

Freidel, David A., & Sabloff, Jeremy A., Cozumel: Late Maya Settlement Patterns, 1984

Hajovsky, Ric,
The Yellow Guide to the Mayan Ruins of San Gervasio, Cozumel, 2012
The True History of Cozumel, 2015

Lothrop, Samuel K., Tulum: An Archaeological Study of the East Coast of Yucatán, 1924

Miller, Arthur G.,
On the Edge of the Sea: Mural Painting at Tancah-Tulum, 1982
The Maya and the Sea: Trade and Cult at Tancah and Tulum, Quintana Roo, Mexico, in The Sea in the Pre-Columbian World, 1977
The postclassic sequence of Tancah and Tulum, Quintana Roo, Mexico, in The Lowland Maya Postclassic, 1985

Morley, Sylvanus G. "The Ruins of Tulum, Yucatan: The Record of a Visit of the Carnegie Institution of Washington Central American Expedition of 1916 to an important but Little Known Maya City." In American Museum Journal, 1917

Ott, Jonathan, The Delphic Bee: Bees and toxic honeys as pointers to psycoactive and other medicinal plants, 1998

Sabloff, Jeremy A., et al, Late Lowland Maya Civilization: Classic to Postclassic, 1986.

Sharer, Robert, The Ancient Maya, 2006

Stephens, John Lloyd, Incidents of Travel in Yucatan, 1843

Vargas Pacheco, Ernesto, Tulum: Organización Político-Territorial de la Costa Oriental de Quintana Roo, 1997

Vale

Made in the USA
San Bernardino, CA
16 July 2018